12-9-60

The Economic Development of POLAND

1919 to 1950

The Economic Development of

POLAND

1919-1950

J. TAYLOR, M.A. (Oxon.)

Department of Economics, The University of Rochester

Cornell University Press

ITHACA, NEW YORK

PRINTED IN THE UNITED STATES OF AMERICA BY
VAIL-BALLOU PRESS, INC., BINGHAMTON, NEW YORK

1154258

With respect and admiration this book is dedicated to

WILLIAM J. ROSE, M.A. (OXON.), Ph.D. (CRACOW)

*Sometime Director of the School of Slavonic and
East European Studies in the University of London*

Parve—nec invideo—sine me, liber, ibis in urbem.
ei mihi, quod domino non licet ire tuo!
vade, sed incultus, qualem decet exulis esse;
infelix habitum temporis huius habe.

—P. Ovidius Naso

Preface

WHEN a small book has been as long in the writing as has this monograph the reader is entitled to an explanation of the delay. Originally, an early—and by now, fortunately, unrecognizable—version was completed by the end of 1944 and then succumbed to the difficulties of publishing in wartime England. Pressure of official duties then compelled me to put the work aside for almost four years. The material was next completely worked over during the summer of 1948 while I was living in New York with only limited access to my reference notes. The version that emerged took until the summer of 1950 to find a hospitable publisher. In the past year, it has been completely rechecked and largely rewritten, mainly in order to incorporate some account of postwar economic planning in Poland. Though the long delay has been frustrating to the author, he feels that it has been of benefit to the reader. It has been possible to check more fully on matters of fact, to remove a certain repetitiousness that marred the earlier versions, and also to relate the subject more closely to contemporary international economic problems. The policies of countries beyond the Communist iron curtain are now, more than ever, matters of more than merely academic interest.

The book deals in some detail with the economic affairs of

a not sufficiently known eastern European country during a period of recent history that was confused in its economics, in its politics, and in those moral values which should always provide the foundations of policy. Events and policies seemed equally chaotic, while expediency rather than considered intellectual judgment or morality only too often regulated the immediate solutions to complex problems. Analysis and reflection on the tangled facts do reveal, however, certain coherent patterns which I have attempted to make clear by setting out as simply and as completely as I could the relevant facts and their background. I have tried to write *sine ira aut studio* of all policies, but particularly of those of which I most disapprove morally (as since 1945).

The structure of the book is simple. After a brief historical introduction to put modern problems in perspective, there follow two short chapters giving the geographical background and some account of the demographic problems of Poland. The first three chapters thus constitute an introduction to the main study, which is contained in Chapters 4 through 11. These eight chapters deal in detail with the economic development of Poland in the twenty years between the wars, that is, from 1919 to 1939. There then follow two chapters which deal with developments from 1939 to 1950. This third part balances the introductory chapters in that it not only rounds off the study by bringing it up to date, but it also provides an economic background for the student of postwar eastern Europe.

The argument of the book is fully documented by statistical tables. These have been based mainly on material provided by three sources: (a) official statistics of Polish governments; (b) League of Nations publications for the period from 1919 to 1939; and (c) United Nations publications for the period from 1939. In the interest of clear presentation, I have not infrequently had to rearrange or amalgamate tables. I have, therefore, felt it important to give precise references for the sources of these tables.

Unfortunately, owing to the loss in transit of some of my research notes, it has not been possible to give the sources of a very few tables. Fortunately, these are among the less important; they will have to be taken on trust.

While a great deal of the source material in this field is highly tendentious—to use a charitable word in place of a blunt one—it is difficult to praise too much the various reports and monographs published by the League of Nations and the United Nations. A list of the most useful will be found at the end of the book.

In the early stages of my researches, I had the advantage of frank criticism of my views by several high officials of the then Polish government. I should particularly like to acknowledge here the help and advice of the following: Dr. F. Zweig, sometime Economic Adviser to the Government of Poland, Dr. Leon Barański, sometime Managing Director of the Bank of Poland, Dr. Bochenski, Dr. Olechnowicz, Dr. Rudzinski, Dr. Waligorwki, and Dr. Zaluski. Above all other help, I must acknowledge the kindly encouragement of Professor William J. Rose, the then Director of the School of Slavonic and East European Studies in the University of London. Without my constant awareness of his kindliness and without his infinite patience in encouraging my interest in Polish affairs, the many difficulties which were encountered at even that early stage would have overwhelmed me. Needless to say, none of the gentlemen named above is in any way responsible for any of the statements or expressions of opinion in this book, which they have not seen even in draft.

With respect to the present book, I am indebted to Mr. Raymond L. Thompson, Vice-President and Treasurer of the University of Rochester, and to Dr. Donald W. Gilbert, Provost of the University, for securing a loan for me from the University to help underwrite the cost of publication. I wish to thank Mr. John R. Russell, Librarian of the University of Rochester, for undertaking the negotiations with Cornell University Press. I have also to thank the anonymous reader of Cornell University Press, whose meticulous comments and queries goaded me into checking and rechecking my sources. I must also acknowledge a debt to the Polish Research and Information Service, New York, an organ of the present Polish government, for supplying some of the material on which the last chapter is based. I feel, however, that they will almost certainly disapprove of the inferences which I have drawn from it and of the general argument of this book, which stresses the very great economic achievements of pre-Communist governments in Poland.

I am particularly grateful to Professor Dexter Perkins, Chairman of the Department of History of the University of Rochester, for his encouraging me to carry on at a time when, because of continuing difficulties, I was inclined to abandon all thought of publication. I am also more grateful than I can readily express to Professor Arthur J. May, also of the Department of History, for his most helpful comments on matters of detail, particularly of literary style, and for acting in general as my scholarly conscience.

Any errors or other sins of omission or commission are, of course, my own, for which I must take full responsibility.

J. TAYLOR

Rochester, New York
June, 1951

x

Contents

LIST OF STATISTICAL TABLES

Part I

THE BACKGROUND

CHAPTER 1

The Historical Background

ANY FRUITFUL study of the economic problems of modern Poland must start by giving consideration to her position during the period of alien rule, which lasted for some 125 years after the late eighteenth-century partition of the country by Russia, Prussia, and Austria. If Poland did not altogether miss the industrial revolution—the most important economic event of the modern world—the abnormal position of the torn and captive country meant that her economic development was twisted, distorted, and retarded to suit the conveniences of the three partitioning powers. For example, at a time when England, France, and Germany were perfecting their railway systems, Russian Poland had only a few strategic railways of no industrial or commercial importance and had not even one modern highway. Economic necessity was deliberately subordinated to the military needs of an alien power. Yet, geographically, Poland is the natural junction for lines connecting the northwest of Europe with the southeast, and the east with the west. So far as means of communication were developed—and for strategic reasons they were deliberately neglected in the frontier regions without regard to the deadening effect on economic life of such a policy—they were systematically orientated toward the centers of the three empires which had dismembered Poland, so that their development, far from assisting the economic progress of the country, tended to intensify the evil economic effects of partition and to make worse the problems which were to face the reborn country in 1920. A further example of the evil economic and social effects of the policies of the partitioning powers was that the credit for the emancipation of the serfs was taken by the three alien governments, who then used it to drive a wedge between the peasantry and the gentry. The evil social effects of this disastrous legacy on a predominantly agricultural country need not be stressed.

Not all the economic effects of incorporation in the partitioning states, however, were bad; for instance, the budding industries of that part of Poland under Russian rule could shelter behind high protective tariffs and at the same time have access to the vast markets of Russia. Indeed, until the beginning of the twentieth century, the chief industrial reservoir of the Russian Empire was Russian Poland, and, although after 1900 the Russian government, by the manipulation of railway charges, discriminated against Polish industries, their position as instanced by the textile industries of Lodz was so firmly established that attack on their superior economic efficiency in the interests of Russia proper was difficult.

To understand the economic position of Poland under the rule of the partitioning powers, it is necessary first to know something of the early economic history of the country. It is not usually realized that the frontiers of the reborn Polish state of 1919 embraced only 35 per cent of the territory included within the 1772 frontiers of the country. While much of the enormous area of mediaeval Poland was thinly populated, especially along the Dnieper, other parts, such as Mazovia, were overpopulated. At the same time important international trade routes crossed the country, and it was toward the end of the fifteenth century that the Polish towns and their burgher classes reached their highest development. This is not the place to go into details of

4

the mediaeval Polish economy, but certain aspects of it must be mentioned if we are to understand the modern economic problems of the country.

In mediaeval times, two important international trade routes crossed at Cracow—one from Flanders to the Genoese colonies on the Black Sea, another from Hungary (where minerals, especially copper, were mined) to the Baltic. The terminus of the water route was originally at Trusso (the present Elbing) but was later moved to Danzig. Polish merchants were very active in the transit trade along these routes, and although in early times exports from Poland were small in volume they were both valuable and important for the mediaeval world, for example, amber for which Poland was the chief source in Europe and tar products for shipbuilding. Cloth and fish were among the main imports. Sandomierz received a Royal Charter conferring on it entrepôt privileges in 1236, and two years later Lübeck merchants established agencies in Danzig which ultimately joined the Hanseatic League in 1366. The export of timber, in the form of shipments of Mazovian wood and later of Carpathian yew, began in the thirteenth century and was followed during the fourteenth century by the export of corn. When the trade route to the Black Sea lost much of its importance owing to the capture by the Turks of the northern shores of the Black Sea, the second route developed considerably in importance. Between 1480 and 1490, some 600 to 700 vessels cleared annually from Danzig. At the same time increasing attention was given to the development of inland navigation, while the continued demand for corn encouraged the development of farming and led to the introduction of the manorial system into Poland in the regions of the lower and middle Vistula. Exports of grain, timber, and cattle through Danzig to the Low Countries, England, and Spain became substantial. The Polish gentry in consequence were becoming wealthy. By the end of the fifteenth century they had begun to encroach on the holdings of the peasants, but the position was not yet acute, and the Polish peasantry enjoyed comparative prosperity.

The economic prosperity of the country was not improved, however, by the war between the Teutonic Knights and Poland or by the accompanying debasement of the currency, a state of affairs unfortunately only too common in mediaeval Europe. Certain towns enjoyed the privilege of minting their own money, and the resulting confusion became so great that foreign merchants would exchange their goods only for ingots of gold or silver.

It was from his observation of this state of affairs that Copernicus, better known as the founder of modern astronomy, formulated in 1526, in his treatise *De monetae cudendae ratio* ("On the Principle of Coining Money"), one of the earliest of economic books, the monetary law that bad money drives out good —a principle which some thirty-two years later was promulgated in England by Sir Thomas Gresham, who gave it the name "Gresham's Law," by which it is still known in economics. The predecessors of Copernicus in this field of study, such as Nicole Oresme, had tended to approach the problem from the moral angle. Copernicus, however, tackled the problem with the precision of scientific analysis, showing that debasement of the coinage is bad economic practice with disastrous economic and social consequences in the form of rising prices. His plan that the minting of money should be a state monopoly, that the quantity of money in circulation should be controlled, that coins of each denomination should contain not less than a certain weight of precious metal, and that the old coinage should be withdrawn when the new was issued was never adopted. It affected too many interested parties who derived profit from the minting of coins or from speculations in the depreciation of the currency.

It is perhaps of more than merely academic interest to compare this episode in the early economic history of Poland with

6

the monetary problems facing the reborn country in 1919 when there were in circulation Russian roubles (Czarist, Kerensky, and Soviet) all of unequal value, Austrian crowns, German marks, and Polish marks (established by the Germans through the Polish State Loan Bank). The problem of speedily establishing a sound currency revealed itself as the most pressing and serious economic question facing the new state, for on its satisfactory solution depended the solution of all the other major economic problems of the new country—even its very survival as a national unit.

We may for our purposes pass over very rapidly the period from the end of the fifteenth century to the time of the partitions. Signs of an unhappy future could perhaps have been discovered by those who cared to look. The peak figure for clearances from Danzig was reached in 1618, and from the middle of the seventeenth century river traffic on the lower Vistula began steadily to decline. By the beginning of the eighteenth century, exports carried downstream were, for the first time, exceeded by imports brought upstream. In the second half of the eighteenth century, the period of state reform brought the appearance of a brighter future, but the action of Frederick II of Prussia in establishing in 1765 a customs house at Kwidzyn (Marienwerder) in order to extort a 10-per-cent ad valorem duty on all goods in transit along the Vistula was a truer augury of the future.

In 1772, war threatened to break out in the Balkans between Austria and Russia, and, since such a war would have been inconvenient to Prussia, that predatory power suggested to Austria and Russia that they should satisfy themselves at the expense of Poland. By the subsequent Treaty of Partition, forced on the Polish Diet by the three powers, Poland lost one-third of her territory and one-half of her population. Frederick of Prussia followed this initial dismemberment by a careful attack on a key point of the Polish economic structure—he decided to ruin Danzig by diverting its traffic to Stettin. His efforts were re-

7

warded with almost complete success. From 1788 to 1793, for political reasons, Prussia pursued a less relentless policy toward Polish trade. In 1793 came the second blow. Austria was absorbed in her war against revolutionary France, and in compensation for her potential gains from France (which never in point of fact came to anything), Russia and Prussia helped themselves to further slices of Poland. The farce was played to its bitter end in 1795 when, by the third partition, Russia, Prussia, and Austria divided the rump among themselves, and Poland ceased to exist as a European state.

Napoleon toyed with the idea of reviving Poland when, partly under the influence of Marie Walewska, he brought into being in 1807 by the Treaty of Tilsit the Duchy of Warsaw, which was joined in personal union to the Kingdom of Saxony and which had Poles on its Council of Ministers. The duchy ceased to exist, however, in 1813 when it was occupied by the Russians after Napoleon's ill-fated Russian campaign.

Although there was some reshuffling of Polish territory, the European settlement at the Congress of Vienna virtually left Austria and Prussia in possession of their spoil. As a concession to the democratic ideas of the western powers, more particularly to those of the British government, the young czar, however, set up in Russian-occupied Poland a semiautonomous vassal state, the so-called "Congress Kingdom."

It was in this area that the foundations of the modern industrial development of Poland were laid. A beginning had been made in this area under Stanislas Augustus Poniatowski, the last King of Poland, and the reform of the Constitution of May 3, 1791, might have effected much in the way of economic development if the unhappy country had been left in peace to work out its own destiny. Nevertheless, after the interruptions of the third partition and the turmoil of the Napoleonic wars, the establishment of the "Congress Kingdom" enabled much to be started. For example, in the years from 1820 to 1840, the De-

8

partment of Mining under the able direction of Minister Staszic began its activities in developing the mineral resources of the country. In the same period, Lubecki, the skillful Minister of Finance, founded the Bank of Poland with the aim of assisting in the industrialization of the country.

The failure of the insurrection of 1830/1831 brought this first attempt at economic development to an end. Though an effort at revival was made during the years 1850 to 1860 in the activities of the Agricultural Association, the defeat of the insurrection of 1863 frustrated again a promising development.

Toward the end of the nineteenth century, however, German immigrants helped to create large business undertakings in Russian Poland where infant industries could shelter behind high protective tariffs and have unimpeded access to the enormous domestic market of Russia. This part of Poland consequently became the chief industrial reservoir of the Russian Empire until about 1900, when the Czarist government adopted a policy of favoring industrial development in southern and central Russia. In spite of these industrial activities, however, Russian Poland remained essentially an agricultural area. The abundance of cheap agrarian labor, provided by a rapidly growing peasant population, made farming profitable even with the primitive techniques used. In this way, the effects of the abolition of serfdom in 1861 were largely nullified for the landowners of Russian Poland.

The most significant aspect of the economic development of Prussian Poland was that the results of the economic policy of the German government were exactly the opposite of its intentions. The main feature of Prussian policy was the organized purchase of Polish lands and the systematic establishment on them of German settlers with the aim of supplanting the entire Polish landowning classes, both great and small. The Commission for Colonization of 1886 had 100,000,000 marks placed at its disposal for the purpose of buying up Polish estates and settling on them "Germans with German wives, not Polish ones." The Poles learned from their enemies, however, and bought more than they sold. The sharp competition for the possession of land forced the price up, and a considerable increase in the prosperity of the countryside was the by-product of the struggle. Wealth enabled mechanical improvements and scientific methods to be applied to farming so that the soil of Prussian Poland, of a somewhat inferior quality by nature, became the best-tilled soil in Poland with the highest average yields. Moreover, those landowners and farmers who were forced out of agriculture emigrated to the towns to set up in trade with the assistance of the capital which they had obtained by the sale of their land. Thus the results of a policy designed to uproot the Poles were relative economic prosperity and a much-needed strengthening of the relatively weak Polish middle classes.

Compared with the parts of Poland under Russian and Prussian rule, Austrian Poland was relatively backward economically, —so much so, indeed, that the phrase "Galician misery" became a common catchword. So far as fiscal and economic policies were concerned, the first fifty years of Austrian rule were purely predatory. The aim of the Hapsburg government was to keep the Polish provinces primarily agricultural in order to serve as a granary for the rest of the Hapsburg empire and as a never-failing market for the produce of Austrian industries. The Austrian attitude toward Galicia in this period was very reminiscent of the British attitude toward its American colonies in the mercantilist era. It led to similar political strains, apart from the complicating factor of nationalistic differences.

Even after the grant of self-government to the Polish provinces in 1867, the economic situation did not change much, for the governing class of Polish country gentry had no sense of the importance of industrial development and readily acquiesced in the purely agricultural destiny which Austrian economic policy assigned to the Polish provinces and which at the same time coincided with the gentry's class interests. This attitude was to leave a difficult economic legacy for the new Poland, since the Galician governing class showed no desire to uplift the decayed state of their towns or to foster the growth of a really strong Polish middle class. Neither did they show any interest in the corporate welfare of the peasantry who made up the bulk of the population. Yet "Galician misery" could be removed only by the development of industries on the model of those of western Europe, and after the abolition of serfdom in Austrian Poland in 1848 it seemed inevitable that sooner or later peasant proprietors would replace the country gentry as the predominant social class. Toward the end of the nineteenth century, however, in spite of the discouragement caused by the collapse of the "oil boom"—an attempt to use the savings of the population, accumulated in the central savings bank of the province, for the development of the oil fields on the northern slope of the Carpathians—some progress was made in developing industry, notably through the League of Assistance to Industry. Progress was particularly marked after 1908.

The economic effects of this unhappy period in Poland's history may be summed up by saying that, although under the partitioning powers a certain measure of economic progress was achieved in certain parts of the country, the economic development of other areas was deliberately retarded, for example, German railway policy was definitely aimed at drawing as much of Poland's trade as was possible into the orbit of Hamburg, Bremen, and Stettin with a consequent decline in the importance of Danzig as a port—a continuation of the policy started by Frederick II. Lwów, however, from the nature of its geographical position, developed considerably as a railway center and had an important textile industry. Naturally, however, no regard was paid to the normal development of the Polish lands as an economic whole, with the result that when the Polish state again came into being, it was divided into areas of uneven economic development with its lines of communications, areas of industrial development, and market areas other than they would have been if the country had been allowed to develop naturally in accordance with is native resources and needs and if its economy had not been truncated and distorted to fit into the economic pattern of the three alien partitioning powers.

When the Polish state was reborn at the end of the first World War, economic revival was made even more difficult by the effects of six years of war from 1914 to 1920. Western Poland was particularly affected. During the first World War, it had been a battlefield for the Russian and Austro-German armies; during 1918 and 1919 the southern areas were disturbed by fighting between the Polish and Ukrainian military formations; and during 1919 and 1920 it was the scene of war between Poland and Soviet Russia. Some idea of the effect of war on the country can be gleaned from the fact that during this period Polish agriculture suffered the loss of over a million and a half farm buildings, while livestock was reduced by one-third. In addition, large areas had been drained of their man power, partly by conscription, partly by enforced wartime emigration. A vivid picture of the state of Poland in those terrible years is given by Sir Stephen Tallents, a member of the British Mission to Poland, who writes in his reminiscences: "In parts of Eastern Poland there was famine that winter. There successive armies, swaying to and fro, had stripped the countryside of food and agricultural gear. Many of the villages had been burnt. The land had lain uncultivated for several years, and the people were living on roots, grass, acorns, and heather. They had little clothing left and no boots or shoes. . . ." [1] Thus when the new Polish state had to face its economic problems, it had to cope with a situation in which the natural economic development of a country had been twisted, distorted, and retarded by 125 years of foreign rule and in which the damaging results of that burden had been intensified by six years of bitter fighting over the countryside and in the towns.

[1] *Man and Boy* (London: Faber and Faber, Ltd., 1943), p. 265.

CHAPTER 2

The Geographical Background and Communications

POLAND, in point of area the eighth state in Europe in the period from 1919 to 1939, has no natural frontiers to east or west, yet from its geographical position the "Polish isthmus" controls vital communication routes between the Black Sea and the Baltic. This basic geographical fact has resulted in variations from time to time in the area known as Poland. The Poland of the twentieth century, for example, is a good deal smaller than the Poland of the sixteenth century, and it is with this smaller area (389.7 thousand square kilometers before the Nazi-Soviet partition of 1939) that we are concerned in the greater part of this book. It may be noted that Poland today (1951), including the former Free City of Danzig and parts of former German territories, but excluding territories ceded to Soviet Russia, is slightly smaller in area than in the years between the wars. It has an area of 311,730 square kilometers.

This central position in Europe by which Poland was made, as it were, into a natural bridge between west and east might have been expected to have resulted in Poland's becoming a great center of trade and industry. This potential economic advantage, however, was offset by the lack of easily defensible natural frontiers, which laid the country open to foreign aggression. Wedged between the huge bulks of the U.S.S.R. to the east, of Germany to the west, with East Prussia, Lithuania, and Latvia to the north and northeast, and with Czechoslovakia and Rumania to the south and southeast, it can be seen that vis-à-vis her neighbors, economically as well as politically, Poland was placed in a delicate situation which demanded a nice balancing of conflicting interests.

Although Poland was often said to be essentially the country of the Vistula (for the basin of that great river covered 62.2 per cent of the area of the Poland of 1919 to 1939), to leave it at that is to oversimplify. Taking a broad view, we find in Poland four main geographical areas which can clearly be distinguished from each other by their physical characteristics and by the economic and social structure arising from those natural foundations. They are: (1) the Northern Lake Belt, (2) the Central Lowlands, (3) the Southern Uplands, and (4) the Carpathians.

The Northern Lake Belt, an area of lakes, marshes, and forests, including the line of moraines known as the Baltic Heights, is essentially a border country. This belt of difficult country (Mazuria) is important in explaining the historical separation of Poland from the Baltic, for it is only where the Vistula has broken through this natural barrier that the Poles reach the Baltic coast, as in Pomorze (the famous "Polish Corridor") where 90 per cent of the indigenous population are Polish.

The Central Lowlands, which cover half the total area of the country, possess soils of varying fertility, and, though generalization is difficult, it may be said that they are inferior to those of the Southern Uplands. Rye and potatoes are thus the distinctive crops of this region rather than wheat and sugar beets. The Central Lowlands include the region of the middle Vistula, which, with Warsaw as its focus, clearly forms the nucleus of modern Poland. This was, over most of its history, an area of many small peasant proprietors with a high density of population (more

14

than 200 to the square mile) and with a high proportion of arable land (from 60 to 75 per cent). The standard of cultivation, however, is not as high as in western Poland, and the crop yields are lower. Thus the area is overpopulated from the economic point of view. Warsaw itself (with 1,300,000 inhabitants before 1939), apart from its importance as the administrative and commercial capital of the country, became important industrially because of its manufacture of textiles and machinery.

The western division of the Central Lowlands (Wielkopolska or Great Poland) centers in Poznan. This area was the cradle of Polish nationality—the ancient city of Gniezno dating from the sixth century. Waterways provided fish and means of communication, while the various soils, including the famous "black earth" of the Kujawy region, provided a firm basis for agricultural prosperity. The existence of salt deposits, especially around Inowroclaw (accounting for 40 per cent of the total Polish salt production in the years just before 1939), was also of significance in determining the economic importance of the region.

The eastern section of the Central Lowlands (Polesie and Wolyn), with its large stretches of marsh, sand dunes, and forest, as well as rivers which periodically flood over their banks, is one of the "poverty corners" of Europe. Its sparse population is largely self-contained, subsisting on meager crops of potatoes, rye, buckwheat, and oats, and making its own garments from locally grown hemp and flax. The backwardness in every sense of this isolated population was one of the main problems facing the new Poland in 1919. It was a problem which could be solved only by something approaching a revolution in the economy of the region, which required drastic changes in the land system, in drainage, and in marketing methods if it was to have a healthy economy. The poverty of the new republic, however, was such that other social and economic needs had to be given priority. Eventually, however, a great scheme for the economic development of Polesie was started in 1931. Of the necessary expenditure 90 per cent came from the central government and only 10 per cent from the region itself, as it was too poor to pay more —a striking measure of its economic backwardness.

The Southern Uplands may perhaps be considered the most important of the four divisions. The soils are varied and rich, which make the region one of dense agricultural population. The southwestern part is made up of the rich Silesian region with its coal, lead, and zinc. The deposits of silver, lead, and zinc have been worked since mediaeval times. There are also some very limited supplies of iron ore, but the iron content is low. Coal is now the chief mineral to be found in the region. The Silesian coal field is second in importance on the Continent only to the great Westphalian coal field and is of fundamental importance in the economic development of the country in modern times.

The southeastern division of the Southern Uplands presents a great contrast to Silesia. In place of a teeming region of modern industry, we find an open, cultivated terrain, treeless and hedgeless, where rural life has changed little in centuries. There is a dense population (between 225 and 300 to the square mile before 1939) of peasant proprietors cultivating grains and root crops, especially wheat and sugar beets, on their small and scattered holdings. It may well be argued, however, that the population of the area was too dense for the maintenance of a reasonable standard of living in spite of the general richness of the soil.

The focal point of the southeast was Lwów (now annexed by the Soviet Union), a center of trade routes, placed where the meeting of two chalk escarpments dominates the convergence of the three great river systems of the Dniester, the San, and the Bug. A measure of the economic significance of its position is given by the fact that nine separate railway lines meet there, and, with a population of 312,000 it was the third city of Poland, ranking after Warsaw and Lodz. Its considerable Jewish population (24 per cent in 1931) played an important part in its commercial development.

The most complex unit of southern Poland is the plateau of Little Poland (Malopolska). In this region, the landscape, with its forests and swamps, resembles the northern lowlands. Good soil is found in some areas of the region, however, while the dense forests and unattractive soils of the Swiety Krzyz (Holy Cross) massif form a natural boundary with the Mazovian region centered on Warsaw. To the southwest a natural boundary is provided by the limestone escarpment stretching from Czestochowa southeastward toward Cracow. In earlier times wood from the neighboring forests was used to work the iron ore, and the area still supplies a certain amount of ore for the blast furnaces of Silesia. The most important towns of the region are Czestochowa (138,000 inhabitants before 1939), manufacturing textiles, paper, and iron and steel, and Cracow (251,000 inhabitants before 1939). The site of Cracow, controlling the narrow corridor between the Carpathian foothills and the southern end of the plateau of Little Poland, favored its growth as a commercial center.

Our last region, the Carpathians, covered only about 4 per cent of the total area of the Poland of 1919 to 1939 and is important for its economic potentialities rather than for actual economic achievements. We should not overlook the fact, however, that in the period immediately preceding the second World War Poland built hydroelectric stations at Roznow and Czchow on the River Dunajec below Nowy-Sacz and at Myczkowce on the River San, while another hydroelectric station was under construction at Porabka on the River Sola where the reservoir was intended also to prevent flooding and to maintain the level of the river at a navigable level on its lower stretches. The Carpathians, which in the High Tatra rise to 8,125 feet—the highest point in Poland—provide a great national park and forest reserve. They form a center for tourist traffic, particularly around

17

Zakopane, while the headstreams of the various rivers, particularly of the Vistula, provide a large potential reserve of water power.

One unfortunate economic legacy of the partitions of Poland was in the sphere of communications. The natural lines of communication are east and west and north and south. Under the rule of the partitioning powers alien interests were dominant with the double result that in some areas, for example, Eastern Poland, communications were completely neglected, while in other areas such communications as were developed stressed an east-to-west organization of Polish commerce and neglected lines of communication from north to south. From the point of view of the economic prosperity of the area, the development of communications north and south as well as east and west was clearly necessary. Since it was not in the interests of the partitioning powers, however, and indeed from their point of view would have had undesirable military consequences, it was not accomplished. The way in which this influenced the development of Polish commerce may be judged from Table 1. This

TABLE 1. EXTERNAL TRADE OF POLISH TERRITORIES (1913).*

	Trade between Polish provinces		Foreign trade, other than with partitioning powers		Trade with partitioning powers	
	Million zl.	%	Million zl.	%	Million zl.	%
Imports	500	8.2	516.8	8.5	5,089.3	83.3
Exports	500	6.5	581.0	7.9	6,268.7	85.6
Total	1,000	7.4	1,097.8	8.1	11,358.0	84.5

* *Source:* Adapted from Casimir Smogorzewski, *Poland's Access to the Sea* (London: Allen & Unwin, 1934), p. 240, table.

table is based on calculations made by E. Kwiatkowski, Minister of Industry and Commerce for many years before World War II, whose role in developing the Polish economy in the 1930's it is almost impossible to overemphasize. It may be seen that there was relatively little trade among the dismembered parts of Poland, for imports and exports alike were virtually monopolized by the partitioning powers. German policy, in particular, by the construction of the Bydgoszcz Canal, which diverted traffic on the Vistula from Danzig to Stettin, for example, or the later development of railroads in such a manner as to draw as much of Poland's trade as possible into the orbit of Hamburg and Bremen, resulted in particularly trying legacies for the revived state in its first years after 1920.

As early as 1834 the position was proving so difficult that the merchants and bankers of Warsaw decided to build a Warsaw-Vienna railroad in order to open a way to the Adriatic and the Mediterranean via the Austrian railroad system, since Prussian policy was barring access to the Baltic. The line was completed in 1848 and became Poland's main commercial link with western Europe.

It might have been thought that even if the development of railway communications had been stunted and distorted by the policy of the partitioning powers, the natural geographical conditions of the country would have provided a network of navigable waterways which could not easily be affected by political factors. This was not so. The network of waterways in central Poland, an area naturally well favored in this respect for commercial exploitation, was deliberately neglected for over a century by Russia. Regular navigation of the Vistula stopped at Warsaw. Moreover, the mining and industrial centers of Poland are not favorably located in relation to the natural waterways of the country, for example, coal is mined on the upper reaches of the Vistula on the watershed between the Vistula and the Oder; the heavy metallurgical industries are naturally located in the same area; the textile industries in the vicinity of the Vistula-Warta watershed are far from any possible waterways, while the sub-Carpathian oilfield is quite cut off from the

Vistula basin. Timber was traditionally floated down the Vistula, but even in this connection the economic advantages of the waterways over the railways can easily be exaggerated.

The difficulties arising from the unequal development of the means of communication in the different parts of the country were further intensified by the ravages of war from 1914 to 1920. There was thus a vicious circle—good communications are a necessity for a prosperous economy, but the new state was so poor that it could do little more than repair the worst ravages of war.

Between 1918 and 1936, the Polish Railways constructed over 2,016 kilometers of new lines and in 1935 to 1937 started approximately an additional 500 kilometers. Even so, the total represents less than half the figure (5,645 kilometers) which the Ministry of Communications had decided as necessary to meet the economic needs of the country. By 1938, there were 18,313 kilometers of standard-gauge railway and 2,125 kilometers of narrow-gauge. We can perhaps form a better estimate of the situation by looking at the comparative figures in Table 2.

TABLE 2. LENGTH OF RAILWAY LINE OPERATED IN KILOMETERS PER THOUSAND POPULATION (1936).*

U.S.A.	29.3
France	10.1
Czechoslovakia	8.9
Germany	8.0
Great Britain	6.5
Belgium	6.0
Poland	5.8
U.S.S.R.	4.9

* Source: Concise Statistical Year-Book of Poland, 1939–41, p. 85, table 5.

Although some 11,613 kilometers of highways were in construction between 1924 and 1936, roads were still sadly deficient, especially in the northeast and east. A natural reason for this was the shortage of stone suitable for road building. The backwardness was greater than it need have been, however, because of the deliberate neglect of the Russian government before 1914. Navigable waterways played an unexpectedly small part in transport. Therefore, in spite of their many deficiencies, the railroads had to bear the main burden of commercial transportation.

Motor and air services were developed, and to a small extent compensated for deficiencies in other types of transportation. The development of motor traffic, however, was held back by the poor roads, while air services, although their development was remarkable, provided no real substitute for adequate railways and waterways.

A very important development, adding a valuable north-to-south route to the previously dominant east-to-west ones, was the building of a new railway between Katowice and Gdynia. This line was not only of immense importance for Poland's foreign trade, but it also reduced the distance which coal had to travel from Silesia to the Lodz textile area.

Finally, mention must be made of the very remarkable development of the Polish mercantile marine, which in the period from 1930 to 1939 increased the number of its maritime vessels from twenty-five to seventy-one.

CHAPTER 3

Population

AMONG the countries of Europe in the period from 1920 to 1939, Poland ranked sixth in population, which was approximately half the size of Germany (before the Nazi aggressions) and three-quarters that of France. At the time of the last census (1931), the population was 32,348,100. It was estimated that by January 1, 1939, the population had grown to 34,849,000. These absolute figures taken by themselves have little significance. Certain peculiarities in the growth and distribution of the population are of much greater significance.

In the first place, Poland is a country of young people. Its natural increase (29.9 per cent between 1920 and 1939) has been the highest among the major countries of Europe. Behind all the specific economic problems of the period must be felt, therefore, the pressure of this rapid growth and the significance of its age distribution. Modern Poland had no fear, therefore of lack of an adequate labor supply or of an internally expanding market, two prerequisites of economic progress. As against these economic advantages, however, it must be remembered that the rapid growth of the population accentuated certain difficulties, notably the very grave problem of rural overpopulation.

The average density of the population in 1939 was 89 to the square kilometer or 283 to the square mile (half the corresponding figure—480 to the square mile—for Great Britain). Like most averages, however, this figure does not tell us anything very useful. The position of Poland relative to the other countries of Europe may be seen from Table 3.

TABLE 3. DENSITY OF POPULATION OF CERTAIN EUROPEAN
COUNTRIES (1939).*

Country	Inhabitants per sq. km.
Belgium	275.3
Netherlands	267.7
United Kingdom and Ireland	163.9
Germany	147.9
Italy	141.4
Czechoslovakia	110.4
Hungary	98.0
Poland	89.7
Denmark	86.7
France	76.1
Yugoslavia	63.4
Spain	50.7
Lithuania	49.0
Latvia	29.6
Estonia	24.8
Sweden	15.4
Finland	11.3
Norway	9.5
U.S.S.R.	8.2

* *Source:* Based on Dudley Kirk, *Europe's Population in the Interwar Years* (Princeton: League of Nations, 1946), p. 10, table 1.

Even these relative figures, however, are not so significant as the relative figures for the different regions of Poland, for in this matter Poland revealed more striking contrasts within its borders than perhaps any country in Europe. Although Silesia was among the most densely populated areas on the continent of Europe, with an average in 1931 of 226 inhabitants to the square

kilometer, the marshes and forests of the eastern provinces of
Poland had a population density of less than one-tenth of the
Silesian average. An immediate impression of the relative densi-
ties of the population dependent on agriculture in the various
parts of Poland can be obtained from Table 4.

TABLE 4. RELATIVE DENSITY OF POPULATION OF POLAND DEPENDENT
ON AGRICULTURE (ABOUT 1930).*

Region	Population dependent on agriculture	Density per sq. km.
Central	7,388,000	85.8
East	4,361,000	75.1
South	5,892,000	122.1
West	1,705,000	55.8
Poland (whole)	19,347,000	86.9

* Source: Extracted from Wilbert E. Moore, Economic Demography of
Eastern and Southern Europe (Geneva: League of Nations, 1945), p. 203.

Approximately two-thirds of the total population lived in rural
areas, and one-third (32.3 per cent according to the 1931 census) lived in urban areas. The corresponding figures for Great
Britain were approximately less than 20 per cent in rural areas
and over 80 per cent in urban areas. The "rural bias" of the Polish
population was even greater than these statistics would indicate, since the overwhelming majority of Polish towns were of
small or moderate size. See Table 5, on the following page.
It follows from the size and distribution of the towns that the
village, not the town, was the most significant population group-
ing for the economic and social characteristics of Poland. Even
in Silesia, for example, the most industrialized region of Poland,
the majority of the inhabitants were to be found in the country
districts and not in the towns. With the exception of a number of
large industrial centers such as Lodz, the towns for the most part
were small towns of a strictly local character whose economic

TABLE 5. DISTRIBUTION OF TOWNS IN POLAND (1939).*

Total number of towns (of any importance)	136

Population (1939 estimates)	Number of towns
2,000–10,000	8
10,000–15,000	33
15,000–20,000	18
20,000–30,000	26
30,000–40,000	17
40,000–50,000	6
50,000–60,000	8
60,000–70,000	2
70,000–80,000	2
80,000–90,000	2
90,000–100,000	0
100,000–110,000	2
110,000–120,000	0
120,000–130,000	3
130,000–140,000	2
140,000–150,000	1
150,000–160,000	0
200,000–210,000	1
250,000–260,000	1
270,000–280,000	1
310,000–320,000	1
670,000–680,000	1
1,300,000	1

Towns ranged by population	Percentage of total number of towns
Below 10,000	5.9
10,000–60,000	79.4
60,000–150,000	10.3
Over 150,000	4.4

* Source: Based on tables in the Concise Statistical Year-Book of Poland, 1939–41.

function was to satisfy the needs of a surrounding agricultural area. Generally speaking, therefore, we may say that the economic role of the cities was of secondary importance.

The net reproduction rate of the Polish population in the 1930's was among the highest in Europe. It was exceeded substantially only by Rumania, Yugoslavia, and the U.S.S.R., although some other countries exceeded it slightly. The precise figures are given in Table 6.

TABLE 6. NET REPRODUCTION RATE OF CERTAIN COUNTRIES (ABOUT 1930).*

Country	Net reproduction rate
Poland	1.25
Greece	1.26
Spain	1.27
Netherlands	1.28
Portugal	1.33
Rumania	1.40
Yugoslavia	1.45
U.S.S.R.	1.72

* Source: Extracted from Kirk, Europe's Population in the Interwar Years, p. 56, table 7.

In considering the economic development of Poland in the interwar period, it is important to bear this pattern of population growth in mind. It had its good aspects, but in important areas it greatly accentuated the agrarian problem, while for the country as a whole it meant that the "Malthusian devil" was very real. When this is realized, added significance is given to the speed at which industrialization was pushed ahead. Agrarian reform and rapid industrialization were the heart of the Polish economic problem in the interwar period, and they come properly into focus when they are seen against the background of the continuous pressure of population on the means of subsistence.

Part II

THE ECONOMIC DEVELOPMENT, 1919 to 1939

CHAPTER 4

The Basic Problems

BEFORE we examine in detail the various aspects of the Polish economy in the period from 1919 to 1939, it would be as well to glance briefly at the main general problems which dominated economic policy and development in these years, since otherwise there is a very real danger of our being unable to see the forest for the trees. The essential nature of Poland's economic problem was precisely expressed in July, 1941, by H. Strassburger, the then Minister of Finance, when he said: "Poland has the population of an industrial country and the economic structure and degree of industrialization of an agricultural country." It has been shown in the preceding chapter that the "Malthusian devil" was a very real one for Poland in the interwar period. With the exception of the U.S.S.R., the rate of increase of the Polish population was the highest of the major countries of Europe. At the same time, Poland lacked the resources and economic organization to provide a decent living, even on a level of bare sufficiency, for a large proportion of its population. It has been estimated that just before the outbreak of war in 1939 at least a quarter of its people were living close to starvation. A striking example of the low level of the peasants' standard of living was the great increase in potato cultivation during the years of economic depression from 1929 to 1935. The explanation was that the peasant could grow enough potatoes to keep himself and his family alive, that is, just not starving, but he could not have maintained this bare subsistence level if he had grown rye or wheat. Again, the national income per head in 1929 was far lower than the corresponding figures for Great Britain, France, or Denmark. The only lower figures were for such notoriously low-standard countries as Bulgaria, Greece, China, and India.

To emphasize the poverty of Poland is not to impugn the economic capabilities of the Poles: it is merely to indicate the enormous difficulties with which they were faced. Moreover, for reasons which will be given in detail in a later chapter, Poland was more dependent than were other countries of eastern and southeastern Europe on the efficient and free working of a prosperous world economy. The trend toward autarchy or national self-sufficiency in economic affairs, which became prevalent in world economic history in the period between 1919 and 1939, was thus disastrous for Poland. Needing to export in order to import and thus obtain the equipment and material for industrializing the country, needing to borrow abroad in order to obtain capital, needing freedom of emigration to other countries in order to help deal with the basic problem of severe overpopulation, the Poles found that the prerequisites for the solution of their economic difficulties were denied them. Forced back, in spite of themselves, to live and organize their economy on a basis of autarchy, they then found that internal maladjustments were intensified and that a difficult problem was transformed into an impossible one.

As we have seen, during the 125 years of alien rule, Poland had been very imperfectly industrialized, so that, quite apart from the havoc and devastation of war, when Poland recovered her freedom, all that she had industrially was the nucleus of the following industries: petroleum, textiles, metallurgy, sugar, and mining. At the same time commercial relations with the market areas of the partitioning powers had naturally been violently severed. It is scarcely an exaggeration to say that Poland passed straight from the conditions of an eighteenth-century rural economy to face the economic problems of twentieth-century industry and commercial competition. The correction of the abnormally uneven distribution of the population between those engaged in agriculture and those engaged in industry and commerce was a basic and urgent problem facing every Polish government after 1919. Its solution involved carrying through an agricultural revolution within the country, creating *de novo* an industrial and commercial system, and carrying on a search for markets abroad, at the same time stimulating a vast potential internal market. And all this had to be done after the country had been torn apart and ruled by three hostile alien powers for nearly 150 years, after the ruin wrought by six years of war, against a background of foreign hostility or at best of indifference, and on the foundations of a predominantly peasant country with only a primitive economic organization.

If we look on finance as a means rather than as an end in economics, that is, as a necessary auxiliary to the efficient working of the economic machine, and so consider its problems apart, we may say that the basic economic problems of Poland between 1919 and 1939 were: (1) rural overpopulation; (2) industrial underdevelopment; (3) the development of the towns and their reintegration with the rest of the national economic system; (4) the revival and direction of international trade as a means of solving the other problems. A complete solution of any one of these problems was, of course, bound up with a solution of each of the others. The problems were all so closely interrelated that the mutual interaction of the steps taken for their solution had to be most carefully considered in order to

31

avoid the disproportionate development of any one sector of the national economy. Moreover, their solution was complicated by the impact on them of the following factors:

1. The economic aspects of the Jewish question;

2. The effects of the economic foreign policies of other countries, for example, the restrictions on immigration into the United States, Brazil, and the British dominions;

3. The effects of the customs war with Germany from 1925 to 1934;

4. The impact on the Polish economic system of the world economic crisis of 1929 and the immediately following years;

5. After the rise of Hitler, the economic problems presented by the military necessity of developing certain areas and sectors of the national economy more rapidly and more intensively than would have otherwise been the case.

Finally, in view of the traditional market orientation of Poland's principal industries, the closing of the Russian market due to the autarchic policy of the U.S.S.R. was catastrophic.

The chronological trend of Poland's economic life in this period was five years of unstable monetary conditions and of inflation; six years of relatively stable currency and increasing prosperity; four years of fighting the effects of the world economic depression; five years of slow but sure economic recovery; then the crashing obliteration of war and successful invasion by Poland's ancient enemies.

The methodological trend of the national economy over the same period was toward *étatisme* or national economic planning. The reason for this state of affairs is fairly obvious. In a relatively undeveloped and economically backward country, private initiative and private enterprise were inadequate for carrying through the drastic but necessary economic revolution which was required. The Poles, for example, showed remarkable thrift throughout the period, but the initial economic standard of the country was so low that voluntary saving was quite inadequate to provide sufficient capital for industrialization. Yet without extensive and rapid industrialization not a single one of the country's major economic problems could be solved. Such a dilemma demanded solution, irrespective of political or philosophical prepossessions or prejudices about private enterprise, state control, or nationalization. In such a situation, what could any responsible government do but pursue a policy of *étatisme?* In short, the economic situation of the new Poland created conditions and revealed problems more akin to those of mercantilism or the state direction of economic policy as practiced in western Europe during the sixteenth to eighteenth centuries than to the conditions and problems of the period of laissez faire and free enterprise. It is important to keep this general background in mind when we assess the solution adopted by any particular Polish ministry for any specific problem of economic policy in the period from 1919 to 1939. Otherwise, we may easily find ourselves applying tests which are not really appropriate and so reaching erroneous conclusions. The economic problems of Poland were essentially those of an underdeveloped country, and in such conditions the simple application of the canons of classical and neoclassical orthodoxy can lead to strangely irrelevant policy conclusions. Alexander Hamilton rather than Adam Smith was the appropriate guide.

CHAPTER 5

Public Finance, Banking, and Investment

ONE of the most interesting aspects of Polish economic development from 1919 to 1939 is the close interlocking of problems of public finance, currency, banking structure, and investment policy.

It is not always possible to separate these problems. Indeed, it is not desirable to do so overrigidly, for the key to the dynamics of Polish economic development in this period is the linking up of private and state enterprise in order to carry through a joint investment policy for the accomplishment of the industrialization of the country. In the early part of the period (before 1930, approximately), this partnership was a forced one resulting from the obvious economic needs of the country. It was adopted with misgiving because it was contrary to the teachings of orthodox laissez-faire economics. In a sense it may be called the triumph of expediency over principle. After the impact of the world economic depression on the Polish economic system, however, the desirability of a joint investment policy, formed by the linking up of the resources of private enterprise and of the state to form part of a consciously integrated plan for the economic development of the country as a whole, was deliberately accepted. In this later period, we may say that theory not only caught up with the march of events, but that, more and more, it consciously took control as Poland became the leading example in Europe of national economic planning on the basis of democratic control. The maximum private incentive possible within the overriding claims of the national economic interest was allowed. In this respect, Poland has a good claim to being the earliest of the modern "mixed economies" like the British economy after 1945.

For the purposes of this chapter, the twenty years between 1919 and 1939 may be divided broadly into four periods, of which each represents a different phase of development. They were:

(1) 1919–1926, a struggle for sheer economic survival, focusing mainly around currency and budgetary problems.

(2) 1927–1930, from the Stabilization Loan to the advent of the world economic crisis. The new state had established itself economically and could now begin to advance on the economic front.

(3) 1930–1935, the impact of the world economic crisis and a second struggle for mere economic survival.

(4) 1935–1939, a period of renewed economic advance and the conscious acceptance of planned capital development.

When the new republic came into being in 1919, it found four different currencies in existence within its territory. They were:

(1) Russian roubles. These were of three kinds, of unequal value, depending on whether they had been issued by the Czarist, Kerensky, or Soviet governments.

(2) Austrian kronen.

(3) German marks.

(4) Polish marks. These had been issued by the Germans through the "Polish State Loan Bank" and were taken over by the new government.

Though the confusion was lessened in 1920 when the Polish

mark became the only legal tender, the real problem was not made any the less acute by this change, for the depreciated mark currency was constantly descending to lower and lower levels as a result of economic instability (which again was accentuated in a self-perpetuating spiral effect resulting from an unstable currency) and of the government's failure to balance the budget.

The root cause of the trouble was that in a war-shattered economy the Sejm (the Polish legislature) kept pressing for expenditure in accordance with its program of social legislation. Consequently, the budget never could be balanced. Indeed, it could not even be constructed for a period longer than one month at a time. To meet the successive deficits, more and more paper money was issued until, by September, 1921, the dollar-mark exchange rate was at more than 6,500 marks to the dollar. Drastic measures were obviously called for and to meet the situation the Finance Minister, Professor Michalski, was given almost dictatorial powers. His remedies were:

(1) The intensification of the production of the country. The government was to provide assistance in achieving this basic aim.

(2) Strict economy in the public administration, especially reductions in the civil service and the army.

(3) The imposition of a capital levy (the *danina*). When the capital levy was actually authorized by the Sejm, there were, however, provisions made for considerable exemptions which deprived it of much of its efficacy.

After an interlude of a few months, the flood of inflation began again, and as milliards of new paper marks poured from the presses the Witos ministry proved unable to control the situation. The salaried and wage-earning classes were long-suffering, but eventually in November, 1923, economic and social discontent flared up into bloody street fighting in Cracow. It was one of the critical moments of the new republic when the structure of the new society might easily have collapsed into anarchy from sheer economic weakness. The crisis revealed, however, one of the great men of modern Poland in the person of W. Grabski to whom the Sejm voluntarily surrendered part of its prerogatives by the law of January 11, 1924, giving the finance minister plenary powers in financial matters with the aims of the "restoration of the Treasury of the State and the reform of the monetary system." Grabski's proposals were both drastic and sweeping. They were:

(1) Increased taxation, including a second capital levy more drastic than that originally proposed by Michalski. This second levy actually proved too severe a drain on the nation's resources, and its later instalments were abandoned. There was also a tax in kind on the owners of forests to provide timber for the reconstruction of villages, a tax which proved extremely unpopular. Moreover, tax administration was to be tightened up, and the collection of taxes was to be rigidly enforced.

(2) Sweeping economies in state administration and severe cuts in public expenditure in order to balance the budget.

(3) The transfer from the central government to local authorities of certain items of public expenditure which more properly belonged to them.

(4) The raising of loans up to a total of half a million gold francs.

(5) The sale, up to the value of one hundred million gold francs, of certain state industrial and commercial undertakings.

(6) The reorganization of the temporary government credit institutions which had been responsible for the issue of the old paper money and their replacement by the Bank of Poland as a bank of issue with a capital of one hundred million gold francs to be provided by public subscription.

(7) The foundation of the Bank of National Economy as a government credit institution to aid postwar reconstruction and the industrialization of the country.

37

(8) The reconstruction of the State Land Bank to fulfill a similar function for agriculture.

(9) The establishment of a new currency with a stable monetary unit—the zloty—which was to equal the Swiss franc on the basis of one zloty to 1,800,000 marks of the depreciated currency.

(10) The conversion and consolidation of former loans to the government and other state obligations.

The period from February, 1924, to November, 1925, was one of almost superhuman activity for Grabski. First, the budget was balanced, and a decree was issued suppressing the issue of marks. On April 14, 1924, the zloty became the sole monetary unit in Poland (from July 1, 1924, it was to be the sole legal tender), and the next day the Bank of Poland was decreed as the Bank of Issue, although it did not actually open for business until April 24. The same month also saw drastic simplification in the state administration and in the reorganization of the state railways on a self-supporting basis. In May, 1924, came the refounding of the State Land Bank with the main purpose of financing the purchase of land by small farmers, the introduction of improvements on their farms, and the liquidation of their debts to private creditors. A fortnight later, on May 30, 1924, the Bank of National Economy came into being. As part of the same reforms, the Post Office Savings Bank was also reorganized.

The success of Grabski's policy was shown by the funding of the "relief" debts contracted after 1918 to the various Allied governments for foodstuffs, machinery, and other essential supplies. The U.S.A. and Great Britain were the largest creditors. In November and December, 1924, funding agreements were reached by which the repayments were to be spread over a period of sixty-two years at a low rate of interest. The international solvency of the new Poland thus seemed assured.

When Grabski met the budget commission of the Sejm on January 19, 1925, he was able to report that his budget expectations for the preceding year had been met and that in point of fact he had achieved a surplus. All was not as well, however, as it seemed on the surface, for the first part of 1925 was marked by heavy unemployment. Grabski had perhaps wanted to move too fast, and his drastic remedies were perhaps too severe for the infant economy. The dearness of money and the lack of credit went along with unemployment and a high cost of living. By stabilizing the zloty at a higher level than was justified by the economic position of the country, Grabski had subjected the currency to a great strain which was accentuated by the poor harvest of 1924 and the consequent heavy rise in the imports of foodstuffs. The next stage is described in a League of Nations report [1] as follows:

The property tax was to be continued for another year. But the 1924 harvest turned out very poor, and for this and other reasons the collection of the tax early in 1925 proved a failure. . . . The deficiency due to the failure of the property tax in the first half of 1925 was filled by the issue of Treasury notes, and the upshot was the new depreciation of the zloty which started at the end of July 1925.

This depreciation created fears of renewed hyperinflation, but in fact it proved relatively moderate. As the exchange declined, the public, expecting the depreciation to continue, reacted as it had done in 1923 by delaying the payment of taxes, and consequently the budget deficit increased further during the second half of 1925. . . .

Grabski attempted to deal with the situation, but failing to obtain from the Bank of Poland the assurances which he thought were necessary for stopping the fall in the value of the zloty he resigned on November 13, 1925.

[1] *The Course and Control of Inflation* (League of Nations, 1946), pp. 26, 27. This report appeared after this chapter had been written. Fortunately, its facts and conclusions coincide with those already reached by the author. No substantial rewriting seemed necessary, therefore, but the report is strongly recommended for readers who have a particular interest in the relations between foreign exchange rates and budgetary deficits.

Grabski's resignation was the prelude to two years of acute economic depression. Inflation and the consequent rising price level had meant a boom in trade, especially in industries working for the export market. The state had been lavish in subsidies, and under the influence of this double incentive of government aid and a rising market there had come about the continuous foundation of new industries. The deflation which followed Grabski's reforms led first to a crisis and then to a severe and prolonged depression. The zloty fell to half the value established by Grabski and became stabilized *de facto* at this level— which in due course enabled recovery to take place by removing the burden of an overvalued currency from the export industries. In the short run, however, not only had Polish industry to suffer from the adverse effects of a deflationary policy, but the rapid fall in the exchange value of the zloty during 1925 damaged Polish credit in the international money market so that such small foreign loans as could be obtained, for example, from Italy and the U.S.A., could be raised only on ruinous terms. Moreover, in some cases, important national assets had to be traded away on unfavorable terms, for example, the state match monopoly to a Swedish company.

Apart from the one contentious issue of the rate of exchange at which he had attempted to stabilize the zloty, Grabski's example was followed by his successors with profit. The firmness with which the budget was kept balanced after 1926 maintained the currency in a condition of very satisfactory stability, and the reserves which were accumulated in the Treasury during the period from 1926 to 1929 helped to cover the inevitable budgetary deficits in 1930 to 1931 which followed the falling off in public revenue resulting from the impact of the world economic crisis on the Polish economy.

In 1926, a commission of American experts, headed by Professor E. W. Kemmerer of Princeton University, visited Poland at the government's request, and, after a period of intensive investigation into the finances and economic conditions of the country, produced a series of valuable reports. The government paid full regard to the advice of these outside experts, an American financial adviser was appointed, and in October, 1927, the Polish government negotiated a foreign loan, while an international stabilization credit was arranged for the Bank Polski. This so-called stabilization loan was an international bankers' loan, the leading roles being played by the Bankers' Trust Company and the Chase National Bank of New York and by Lazard Brothers and Company of London. It amounted to $62,000,000 plus two million pounds sterling. It was issued at 92 and bore interest at 7 per cent. Thus, the terms were far from generous. At the same time a group of fifteen European central banks and the Federal Reserve system granted the Bank of Poland a stabilization credit of about $20,000,000. The Polish banking system was thus brought out of isolation and linked with the leading international money markets.

These credits enabled the zloty to be stabilized. It was put on a gold basis of 1 zloty $= \frac{1}{5,924.44}$ kg. of pure gold. The old currency was at a parity of $\frac{172}{100}$ of the new, that is, approximately 58 per cent. At the same time, the capital of the Bank of Poland was expanded from 100 to 150 million zloty. One half of the small treasury notes—of which the excessive issue had been one of the causes of the fall in the value of the zloty in 1925—was retired from circulation, and provision was made for converting the rest into silver coin. The floating debt of the Treasury was paid off, and 75,000,000 zloty were allotted to reserve. Finally, 140,000,000 zloty were assigned to economic development.

In consequence, the period of 1927 to 1928 was one of constructive government investment on an unprecedented scale. The budget for 1927 to 1928 showed a surplus of 214 million zloty, and in addition 51 million zloty had been transferred to increase the capital of the State Land Bank. Of the surplus, 88 million zloty were devoted to public works and 45 million invested in standard securities. The rest was held as current reserve. The following year showed a further surplus of 200 million zloty, but then came a check since as a result of the economic crisis the rapid growth of revenue ceased. In 1929 to 1930, the intake of revenue was approximately the same as the preceding year. The world economic depression had a serious effect on the revenues of the Polish government, as may be deduced from the following salient facts: taxation brought in about the same as the previous year, and so did the state monopolies; state forests were up to the income estimated; posts and telegraphs actually did better; but the state railways were unable to hand anything over, whereas the budget estimate had been for a surplus of 40 million zloty. Customs duties were the most affected by the crisis, for as the purchasing power of the country declined so did imports of manufactured and semimanufactured goods. The next few years saw a series of deficits, though these were sometimes concealed as in the budget for 1935 to 1936, when an actual deficit of nearly 250 million zloty was hidden by transfer from the national loan of 1933. The emergence of the country from the economic depression and the beginnings of prosperity were first seen in the budget for 1936 to 1937 when a surplus of 50 million zloty was estimated.

In this period successive Polish ministries and the banking system followed a policy of great orthodoxy and financial rectitude. This action has won praise from outside experts, as witness the following comment:

The experience of Poland also deserves special mention. Poland was one of the few countries that succeeded in enforcing a severe monetary deflation in the face of foreign credit withdrawals while maintaining the gold value of the currency without any general exchange control up to April 1936. But the deflation came about without much active pressure from the central bank. While the gold and exchange reserve was more than halved during the four years 1930–34, the bank's domestic assets showed little change on balance.

It was the commercial banks which, faced with a loss of cash, played a leading part in the contraction of credit, cutting down their bill portfolio by two-thirds and their advances by one-third over that period. . . .[2]

Within Poland, however, this financial orthodoxy was viewed with somewhat mixed feelings, since the deflation led to continued unemployment and to a relatively slow emergence from the depression. It was argued that Kwiatkowski, the dominant figure in Polish financial and economic policy during these years was mistaken in his stubborn maintenance of the high exchange value of the zloty and in his refusal to join the "sterling bloc."

The dilemma before him, however, was not an easy one. If the exchange value of the zloty was maintained at a high level, it is true, there was a consequent handicap imposed on the export trades. This policy was followed and was no doubt partly responsible for the severe unemployment in Poland at this period. If Kwiatkowski had joined the "sterling bloc" and devalued the zloty a stimulus would have been given to the export trades and—theoretically—there would have been an improvement in the employment position in the export industries, with a consequential creation of secondary employment in other industries and the earlier emergence of Poland from the depression. So it is argued by his critics. The argument is valid if other things can be assumed to have remained equal while these changes were taking place. But does this assumption of *ceteris paribus* hold good? In a country with such painful memories of inflation as Poland and with such a low propensity to save (mainly owing to the initial low level of the national income), the maintenance of public confidence in the currency was of paramount importance for investment policy. If Kwiatkowski had followed a policy of adherence to the "sterling bloc," the concomitant devaluation of the zloty would undoubtedly have

[2] *International Currency Experience* (League of Nations, 1944), p. 82.

shaken public confidence. There might easily have followed another flight from the zloty, and investment would have been very adversely affected. Thus employment would *not* have been stimulated, and the only effects would have been a worsening in the economic position and a depreciation of the people's savings. In view of the peculiar position of Poland in respect to capital accumulation, the balance of judgment probably should go in favor of the policy actually pursued by Kwiatkowski.

Statistical Table 7 shows the changes in the Polish budget during the period under discussion.

Polish banking and finance in the period from 1919 to 1939 had several very unusual and interesting features. These were the result of a dearth of capital and credit on the one hand and the necessity, on the other, for financing: (a) the foundations of the industrialization of the country; (b) vast agricultural reforms; (c) foreign trade, in particular with a view to providing the necessary imports of machinery and raw materials for the industrialization of the country. There was thus a great unsatisfied demand throughout the whole period for capital and credit. The main effects of this peculiar position were two: first, the increasing intervention of the state in banking and investment on a scale previously unparalleled in western Europe, and, second, the presence of an exceptionally high proportion of foreign capital in Polish industry.

A further overriding influence must also be mentioned at this point; namely, after 1927 the fear of a return of inflation limited the circulating media below an economically desirable level and thus further emphasized the ill effects of the initial dearth of credit. The deflationary effect of maintaining the zloty at a relatively high valuation was thus intensified, and economic recovery was retarded. Money remained dear, and so all investment programs were severely handicapped. This fact is strikingly illustrated by Table 8 which shows the comparative rates of discount of the central banks of eight commercially important countries.

TABLE 7. POLISH REVENUE AND EXPENDITURE (1919–1939)
(IN MILLION ZLOTY AT 1934 VALUE).*

Year	Revenue	Expenditure	Balance
1919	856	2826	—1940
1920	526	2469	—1943
1921	561	1248	— 687
1922	998	1070	— 72
1923	774	1736	— 962
1924	2357	2683	— 326
1925	2568	2928	— 360 †
1926	2128	1942	156
1927	2728	2513	215
1928	2988	2819	169
1929	3031	2971	60
1930	2748	2801	— 53
1931	2262	2466	— 204
1932	2002	2174	— 172
1933	2458	2448	10 ‡
1934	2115	2176	— 61 §
1935	2016	2168	— 158 ‖
1936	2217	2213	4
1937	2432	2411	21
1938	2474	2458	16
1939	2526	2526	0 #

* This table has been constructed partly from information in a table in Casimir Smogorzewski, *Poland's Access to the Sea* (London: Allen & Unwin, 1934), p. 245, and partly from information in *Concise Statistical Year-Book of Poland, 1939–41*.

† For fifteen months.

‡ Actual deficit, 337 million zloty.

§ Revenue included 175 million transferred from National Loan.

‖ Budget estimate; actual deficit nearly 250 million zloty.

Budget estimate; actual figures not available.

TABLE 8. DISCOUNT RATES OF CENTRAL BANKS (1928–1938)
(YEARLY AVERAGES).*

Countries	1928	1929	1930	1931	1932	1935	1936	1937	1938
Poland	8.0	8.6	7.2	7.5	7.2	5.0	5.0	5.0	4.5
Belgium	4.3	4.4	3.0	2.5	3.5	2.2	2.0	2.0	2.6
France	3.5	3.5	2.7	2.1	2.5	3.5	3.7	3.8	2.8
Germany	7.0	7.1	4.9	6.9	5.2	4.0	4.0	4.0	4.0
Italy	6.0	6.8	5.9	5.9	5.6	4.2	4.7	4.5	4.5
Rumania	6.0	8.2	9.0	8.3	7.2	4.5	4.5	4.5	3.8
Great Britain	4.5	5.5	3.4	3.9	3.0	2.0	2.0	2.0	2.0
U.S.A.	4.5	5.2	3.0	2.1	2.8	1.5	1.5	1.3	1.0

* *Source:* Extracted from *Concise Statistical Year-Book of Poland, 1939–41*, p. 98, table 11.

If we turn from the price of money to its circulation per person per annum, we find that this same phenomenon of the relative scarcity of money in the Polish economic system is even more strikingly brought out.

TABLE 9. AVERAGE CIRCULATION OF MONEY PER INHABITANT (1935)

Countries	£	s.	d.
Great Britain	8.	8.	0.
Germany	7.	15.	0.
Austria	6.	4.	0.
Czechoslovakia	3.	15.	0.
Rumania	2.	2.	0.
Poland	1.	12.	0.

An important feature of the Polish economy which may be explained by reference to Table 9 is that a high price of money tends to the maintenance of a minimum level of cash balances.

When the reborn Polish state came into being in 1919, the position regarding banking structure and the supply of capital was indeed chaotic. Not only was the monetary system completely disorganized, as has been explained, but the deposits of Polish citizens in the banks and other financial institutions of Russia, Germany, and Austria had melted away to the vanishing point as inflation had increased in those countries. The period of immediate postwar inflation in Poland saw the mushroomlike growth of small speculative banks and ephemeral joint-stock companies, while long-term credit became an almost obsolete institution.

Under Grabski's financial regime, the reconstruction of banking and credit on a more solid economic foundation seemed well underway, but with the renewed collapse of the zloty in 1925 this development was interrupted, and in the course of the financial crisis of that period many credit institutions disappeared while others survived only by the aid of state credits. Capital accumulation was naturally checked by these developments, and after the stabilization of the currency in 1927 it was still some time before confidence could be reawakened and savings in the form of bank deposits revived. During this period there was a tendency for savings to take the form of deposits on dollar account. The state banks after a time began to resume long-term credit operations and the surviving private banks, after their reorganization on financially sound lines by the law of 1928, began to attract savings again and to enjoy foreign credits. Then came the blow of the world economic crisis, particularly severe for mainly agricultural countries such as Poland. Once again the ill effects of a deficiency in the amount of money in circulation, scarcity of capital, and dearth of credit could be seen at work in the Polish economy. Although the bottom of the economic depression in Poland may be placed in 1933, there was some sluggishness in the revival of capital investment. If we take 1928 = 100, the index of investment had fallen to 33 in 1932 but rose to 64 at the beginning of 1937. The stimulus to the revival of investment came partly from a diminution of the tendency to hoard, partly from the effects of the devaluation of the dollar. A reverse effect was brought about, however, by the difficulties of the gold bloc currencies in 1934 to 1935. By June, 1936, the gold reserves of the Bank of Poland amounted to only 380 million zloty, which in the opinion of the government was inadequate to meet the obligations of the foreign debt and to finance the Four-Year Plan. It was hoped that by this plan, which called for investing 1,800 million zloty in railways, roads, bridges, canals, and other public works, unemployment could be conquered in the period 1936 to 1940. Currency control accordingly was instituted, and the transfer abroad of sums due to foreigners holding government bonds and other Polish securities was suspended. Polish securities naturally fell heavily in value in New York and London. Payments due on these securities were to be made through "blocked" accounts expendable in Poland. Settlements abroad were to depend on whether the trade balance with the particular countries was favorable or not. Polish credit abroad had been unmistakably shaken, and the trend toward increasing self-dependence in respect to capital investment was emphasized.

To turn now from the general financial background to details of the banking structure of the country, we may say that the foundations were effectively laid by Grabski's reforms and by the accompanying reorganization of the state banking institutions, as briefly described above. On January 20, 1924, a decree was issued which authorized the foundation of a bank of issue with a capital of 100 million zloty. The shares were taken up as follows:

	Per cent *
Industrial undertakings	33
Agricultural undertakings	8
Co-operative societies	8
Other banks	17
Commercial undertakings	5
Government officials	17
Government institutions	10
Other sources	2

* Source: R. Machray, The Poland of Pilsudski (London: Allen & Unwin, 1936), p. 179.

48

This capital was increased by 50 million zloty after the stabilization loan of 1924. The Bank of Poland, as thus created, was legally independent of the state and was given the exclusive right of note issue for a period of forty years in return for an open credit to the state, free of interest, up to a maximum of 50 million zloty. Notes in circulation were to have 30 per cent cover in gold or foreign exchange and 40 per cent cover by bills of exchange and reserves of metallic currency estimated at its gold value.

During 1924 the bank was feeling its way forward. The following year was one of restricted activity, owing to the second fall in the exchange value of the zloty. The year 1926 saw the beginnings of favorable development, however, and during 1927 and 1928 the credit policy of the bank was more liberal. In 1929 came a check caused by the onset of the world economic crisis. The position of the bank at various dates may be seen from Table 10.

TABLE 10. ASSETS AND LIABILITIES OF THE BANK OF POLAND (SELECTED YEARS).*

Year	Assets						Liabilities	
	Gold	Foreign exchange	Bills	Collateral security loans	Treasury debts	Securities	Notes	Sight liabilities
			(In Million Zloty)					
1928	621	714	641	91	25	45	1295	524
1932	502	137	586	114	90	106	1003	220
1937	435	36	661	24	80	219	1059	360
1938	445	19	831	112	45	223	1406	251

* Source: Extracted from Concise Statistical Year-Book of Poland, 1939–41, p. 96, table 8.

The policy of the bank has been criticized on the ground that the amount of paper money issued was smaller than it should have been in the interests of the proper economic development of the country. It must be remembered, however, that the first duty of the bank was to maintain the standard of the circulating medium. In a country with dreadful memories of the dire miseries of inflation, a conservative policy in regard to note issues was merely common prudence. Moreover, there is the further point that the volume of the bank note circulation in a country depends *inter alia* upon how much cash people want to hold. A central bank must to some extent, therefore, maintain a passive attitude and accommodate its policy to the actual possibilities of the moment. It cannot be guided by an abstract analysis of what may be considered theoretically desirable.

The Bank of National Economy (*Bank Gospodarstwa Krajowego*) was founded as a government credit institution in order to aid the postwar reconstruction and the industrialization of the country. It was established in 1924 by the fusion of three banks—the Polski Bank Krajowy (National Bank of Poland), the Zaklad Kredytowy Miast Malopolskich (South Poland Urban Credit Bank), and the Bank Odbudowy w Malopolsce (Reconstruction Bank of South Poland). The total capital of 150 million zloty was furnished by the state and remained the property of the government. From its foundation up to 1927 the bank assisted all sections of the national economy which were in need. After 1927, however, the bank began to concentrate on long-term credit operations mainly for investment purposes. It also financed the many state enterprises, local government authorities, and agricultural, trading, and building co-operative societies. Most of the reconstruction work in the towns of Poland was carried out with its assistance.

The bank thus became a principal factor in the development of the Polish economic system. The Kemmerer Commission recommended that the bank

50

should become primarily an institution for financing national, state, and municipal enterprises, the central agency for the control and administration of all long-term government funds used in business and should be eventually the only state Bank empowered to issue long-term mortgage bonds. . . . [It] should withdraw from its deposit and loan activities with the general public, leaving that field to the joint stock banks and confining its business within the limits previously outlined.[3]

In spite of these recommendations, however, the state banks, of which the Bank of National Economy was the most important, grew immensely in relative importance when compared with the private banks. This fact, which was the result of the economic problems of developing a new economy, is clearly brought out in Table 11. It should be noted that this table, which is based on information given in the *Concise Statistical Year-Book of Poland, 1939–41*, is not exhaustive. It shows only the *principal* types of credit institutions in Poland during this period.

The second of the state-owned banks was the National Land Bank (Panstwowy Bank Rolny), decreed in 1919, reorganized under the Grabski regime (May 14, 1924), but not coming into being in its fully developed form until 1928. The main purpose of this bank was to finance the purchase of land by small farmers and to assist them in introducing technical improvements on their farms and in paying off their debts to private creditors. The bank financed agricultural co-operatives, had a hand in selling artificial fertilizers from the state factories, and administered state funds allocated to agriculture. In 1933 and 1934, the bank had to bear the main burden of the conversion of both short- and long-term agricultural credits. This burden was so great that the bank had to draw on its reserves and to reduce its paid-up capital. The most important source of its working funds were those supplied by the government (approximately 710 million zloty on December 31, 1937), but it also accepted de-

[3] Kemmerer Commission Reports, pp. 266–267.

TABLE 11. MAIN CREDIT INSTITUTIONS OF POLAND (1928–1938).

Institution	1928	1932	1933	1934	1935	1936	1937	1938
Bank of Poland	1	1	1	1	1	1	1	1
Branches	52	53	53	53	50	50	50	50
Agencies	168	227	227	246	247	247	248	250
State-owned banks	2	2	2	2	2	2	2	2
Branches	32	31	31	32	31	31	32	33
Private joint-stock								
Domestic	55	47	39	35	32	32	26	26
Branches	162	97	84	84	84	81	49	84
Foreign	6	5	5	4	4	4	4	4
Branches	14	13	13	11	10	10	9	9
Post office savings								
banks	1	1	1	1	1	1	1	1
Branches	3	10	9	9	9	9	8	9
Postal agencies	3363	3704	3686	3608	3661	3757	4041	4163
Communal savings	314	377	367	364	363	362	357	353

posits from the public (177 million zloty at December 31, 1937) and deposits from the Treasury (32.4 million zloty at December 31, 1937).

The native thrift of the Polish peasants and industrial workers found an outlet through the post office savings bank. This institution was founded in 1919 and modeled on analogous institutions in other countries, but it was not until 1925 (with the stabilization of the currency) that it began to flourish. Between 1925 and 1928 savings deposits in the bank increased tenfold. The accumulated savings were invested in state securities so as to assist the government in its economic activities in various fields.

Small savings were also encouraged by the founding of communal and district savings banks which had the support of the local government authorities. This form of credit organization had been particularly favored by the small investor in central and eastern Europe before 1914. When the permanent stabilization of the zloty seemed to have been achieved, these local savings banks quickly revived, and a presidential decree in 1927 laid the foundation for their uniform development throughout Poland. Although, in common with all credit institutions, they were affected by the impact of the world economic crisis, they were not so immediately affected as were the private banks. Indeed, in 1930 and 1931, there developed a strong tendency toward the transfer of savings from private banks to municipal and provincial savings banks. The progress of small savings in Poland in this period may be seen from statistical Table 12.

TABLE 12. SAVINGS DEPOSITS IN POLISH SAVINGS BANKS (1928–1938).*

	1928	1929	1930	1931	1932	1935	1936	1937	1938
Total (in million zl.)	447	570	789	891	1027	1331	1304	1517	1570
Per head (in zl.)	14.5	18.2	24.9	27.7	31.5	39.3	38.1	43.9	44.5

* *Source:* Based on *Concise Statistical Year-Book of Poland, 1939–41,* p. 101, table 17.

The rate of increase in savings in Poland in this period was much greater than in many other countries, as may be seen from Table 13. The low absolute total of savings was the result of the poverty of the country and did not reflect the strongly developed instinct for thrift of the Polish people.

In the early years of the new republic, private banking had been brought into some disrepute by the mushroom growth of hundreds of banks started to exploit the monetary confusion

53

TABLE 13. GROWTH OF SAVINGS DEPOSITS IN SAVINGS BANKS
(1930–1936).*

Country	1930	1931	1932	1933	1934	1935	1936
			(1928 = 100)				
Poland	176	200	230	241	277	298	292
France	143	188	212	218	225	229	218
Germany	149	140	141	166	178	187	199
Great Britain	103	106	112	122	131	144	157
Czechoslovakia	114	128	129	122	122	126	126

* *Source:* Constructed from information in *Concise Statistical Year-Book of Poland, 1939–41.*

of the inflationary period. The public at first tended to favor the state banks, but after the clearing away of undesirable elements (between 1923 and 1926 the number of banks and bank offices fell from 834 to 296), the public began to regain confidence in private banks. The Kemmerer Commission in 1926 had expressed the view, "One of the most important problems in Poland to-day is the re-establishment of confidence in the Polish joint stock banks." [4] By 1927, it seemed that the public had regained that confidence, for 35 per cent of savings were deposited in private banks as against 19 per cent in state banks, and in 1928 50 per cent of the short-term credits made were issued by private banks. Although the private banks were still far inferior in capital resources to the state banks, they were becoming less dependent on them. Moreover, there was to be observed the progressive concentration of capital in a few strong institutions, for example, in 1928, of the twenty-nine banks in the National Association of Polish Banks, the four largest attracted more than one-half of all savings. This development of private banking was rudely shaken, however, by the effects of the world economic crisis, which was followed in Poland as in

[4] *Reports,* p. 253.

other countries by many bankruptcies of what had seemed strong and well-organized banks. The result was that the state banks grew enormously in relative importance.

Mention must also be made of the Acceptance Bank (*Bank Akceptacyjny*) of which the entire capital was owned by the state banks and other state institutions. The Acceptance Bank, founded in 1933, had for its main purpose the granting of acceptance credits to those institutions which were engaged in the conversion of short-term agricultural credits. This activity was completed by 1937.

The general layout of the banking structure of Poland and the relative importance of its various parts may be seen from Table 14.

TABLE 14. DEPOSITS IN POLISH CREDIT AND SAVINGS INSTITUTIONS (IN MILLION ZLOTY) (1928–1938).*

Institution	1928	1929	1930	1931	1932	1935	1936	1937	1938
Bank of Poland	451	446	189	196	208	188	237	294	206
Bank of National Economy	325	255	244	238	261	287	378	540	481
National Land Bank	50	68	68	60	100	108	130	178	171
Communal banks	30	30	34	28	29	39	45	59	62
Private banks	866	959	1018	609	512	463	467	556	627
Foreign banks	45	48	43	55	52	48	63	62	75
Postoffice savings banks	315	384	432	510	623	881	896	1038	1094
Communal savings banks	330	404	535	563	587	677	687	495	851

* This table does not include all the credit institutions in Poland. The only sizable institutions omitted, however, are the credit co-operative societies.

Source: Constructed from tables in *Concise Statistical Year-Book of Poland, 1939–41.*

To complete this short description of the credit and savings institutions of Poland, mention must be made of the Polish stock exchanges. Although there had been a Warsaw Stock Exchange as long ago as 1817, which had played its part in the brief industrial development of the Congress Kingdom, stock exchanges were practically nonexistent in the Poland of 1919. By 1921, however, "official quotations" were to be found again, and there took place the legal regulation of stock exchanges on the model of the Austrian exchanges. An important provision governing the operation of the Polish stock exchanges was that there was supervision over each exchange by a government commissioner who had a right of veto on all resolutions of the elective committee which administered the exchange. There were stock exchanges at Warsaw, Poznan, Cracow, Lwów, Lodz, and Wilno. In the ten years before the outbreak of war in 1939, there was a marked decline in the number and value of the transactions carried out on the exchanges.

TABLE 15. TRANSACTIONS AND TURNOVER OF POLISH STOCK EXCHANGES (1928–1938).*

	1928	1929	1930	1931	1932	1934	1935	1936	1937	1938
Transactions (in thousands)	87	69	56	53	50	52	50	51	54	56
Turnover (in million zloty)	917	584	747	1007	685	510	662	531	508	564

* Source: Extracted from Concise Statistical Year-Book of Poland, 1939–41, p. 103, table 21.

The low national income of Poland (with a correspondingly low propensity to save), taken in conjunction with the investment needs of the country both for immediate postwar reconstruction and rehabilitation after 1919 and for long-term capital investment to carry through the industrialization and the reconstruction of the agricultural system, meant that the aggregate sum of savings in Poland was far below the investment needs of the country. Economic development would have proceeded intolerably slowly if it had not been for the influx of foreign capital. This influx has been classified [5] under the following heads:

A. *Government*

(1) The indebtedness of the Polish government toward the governments of other countries

(2) Postliquidation indebtedness to the holders of Austro-Hungarian government bonds

(3) Government loans subscribed by public issue abroad

(4) Long-term loans received by the Bank of National Economy from foreign financial institutions

(5) Commodity credits taken up by the government from foreign undertakings in connection with the delivery of supplies for the needs of the state or state enterprises

(6) Foreign capital which entered the country in connection with the operation of monopolies and concessions for the exploitation of various monopolies

B. *Local government bonds*

(1) Loans subscribed by public issue abroad

(2) Loans accepted from foreign financial institutions

(3) Loans received from foreign undertakings in conjunction with the deliveries of supplies from abroad for the needs of local government boards and their enterprises

C. *Private institutions*

(1) Loans to private long-term mortgage credit associations

(2) Foreign long-term bond issues of private enterprises

(3) Credits granted to private banks

(4) Cash credits granted to industrial and commercial undertakings

(5) Commodity credits granted to industrial and commercial undertakings

[5] The classification is that given by Leopold Wellisz in his standard work *Foreign Capital in Poland.*

(6) Participation by foreign capital in the capital funds of private enterprises

(7) Capital and credits of branches of foreign enterprises operating in Poland

We need only remark here on the cautious policy of the Polish government in raising loans abroad. It always paid scrupulous regard to the relations between its obligations and its ability to meet them. Although this attitude rendered necessary the postponement of much capital investment which might have stimulated employment, it bore its reward in the confidence which continued to be shown in the Polish currency after 1927 and in the fact that Poland was not compelled to resort to foreign exchange controls until 1936.

More important, perhaps, than the influx of foreign capital on the account of the central government and of local government bodies was the influx of capital to meet the needs of private enterprise. The total amount supplied for this purpose slightly exceeded the sum total lent to the state and local government bodies (3,800 million zloty at January 1, 1936 as against 3,600 million zloty). Taking the capital of all Polish joint stock enterprises as a whole, it was estimated that just before the war of 1939 to 1945 foreign capital contributed a total of 38.4 per cent. The largest sums were invested in mining and ironworks, followed by the chemical and electrical industries. In 1931 it was estimated that the industries most affected by foreign investment were public utilities, ironworks, mining, and the chemical industry. Details are set out in Table 16.

The actual amounts of foreign capital invested in the private sector of the Polish economy are shown in Table 17.

It appears from Table 17 that between 1929 and 1935 Polish industry redeemed nearly one-third of the sums invested or advanced by foreign capital in 1929, a very substantial achievement. Foreign capital was associated mainly with the large- and

TABLE 16. INVESTMENT OF FOREIGN CAPITAL IN POLISH
INDUSTRIES (1931).*

Industry	Foreign capital as percentage of whole capital in industry
Ironworks	65.4
Mining	51.9
Gasworks, waterworks, electricity	45.6
Chemical industries	40.6
Communications and telephones	29.3

* Source: Based on R. Dyboski, Poland (London: Ernest Benn & Co., Ltd., 1933).

TABLE 17. INVESTMENT OF FOREIGN CAPITAL IN POLISH INDUSTRIES BY
CATEGORY OF INVESTMENT, IN MILLION ZLOTY (1929–1935).

Year	Short-term bank credits	Cash credits to industry	Commodity credits	Shares in Polish enterprises	Capital and credits of branches of foreign enterprises	Long-term credits	Total
1929	676	1828	1116	1474	366	194	5654
1930	643	1829	525	1654	371	189	5211
1931	401	1884	244	1685	340	317	4871
1932	292	1689	138	1751	326	312	4508
1933	248	1540	122	1754	323	310	4297
1934	259	1262	110	1737	312	284	3964
1935	276	1154	95	1692	301	273	3791

medium-scale industries. When it is remembered that Poland was primarily an agricultural country in which handicrafts and small-scale industry (in which foreign capital had no interest) were, relatively, by far the most important industrial sectors, it

59

will be understood that the role of foreign capital in Polish industry as a whole was not as important as its share in joint-stock and limited-liability companies would indicate.

The order of importance of foreign capital by country of origin is given in Table 18.

TABLE 18. FOREIGN CAPITAL IN POLISH INDUSTRY
BY COUNTRY OF ORIGIN (1937).

Country	Percentage of total foreign capital invested in Polish industries
France	27.1
U.S.A.	19.2
Germany	13.8
Belgium	12.5
Switzerland	7.2
Great Britain	5.5
Austria	3.5
Netherlands	3.5
Sweden	2.7
Czechoslovakia	1.6
Other countries	3.4

The most striking fact in this connection was that the German share had dropped from 25 per cent of the total in 1931 to 13.8 per cent in 1937. Unlike certain Balkan and central European countries Poland had succeeded in avoiding overdependence on the German economic machine.

CHAPTER 6

Agriculture

THROUGHOUT the whole of the period which we are considering, Poland remained an agricultural country in spite of the great strides that were made toward securing a better-balanced economy by pushing ahead with industrialization. This basic fact is well brought out when we consider Table 19 which shows the occupational distribution of the civilian labor force.

TABLE 19. OCCUPATIONAL DISTRIBUTION OF THE POLISH POPULATION IN THOUSANDS (1931).*

Occupation	Rural areas	Urban areas	Total
Agriculture	18,737	610	19,347
Forestry, fishing, and gardening	190	444	634
Mining and industry	2,405	3,773	6,178
Commerce and insurance	458	1,485	1,943
Communication and transport	424	729	1,153
Public service and church	218	495	713
Schools and cultural	125	213	338
Therapy, sanitary services, and social welfare	53	223	276
Domestic service	128	313	441
Other occupations	447	846	1,293
Total population	23,185	8,731	31,916

* *Source:* Based on Polish census returns, 1931.

Just over 27 per cent of the total population lived in urban areas, while just over 70 per cent lived in rural areas. It helps in the appreciation of these figures when we remember that in Great Britain rather more than 80 per cent of the population lived in urban areas. Moreover, we should also bear in mind the important fact that the overwhelming majority of Polish towns were small towns of fewer than 40,000 inhabitants.[1]

Agriculture thus played a predominant part in the economic life of Poland. Its relative importance is quickly realized from Table 20.

The level of the prices of agricultural products in relation to other price levels was, therefore, throughout this period, the key to the dynamics of the economic development of the country. If Polish agriculture was prosperous, purchasing power was available for the consumption of manufactured products. The demand for such products enabled new industries to be created and to prosper. The new industries could absorb the surplus rural population, could deal with "concealed unemployment" in rural areas, and so could increase the standard of living of the whole population—rural as well as urban. This increased standard of living could then give a further stimulus to industrial development and so the cumulative process leading to national prosperity could continue. Agricultural depression, however, such as was caused by the effects of the world economic crisis, could set the spiral operating in reverse and lead cumulatively to national economic disaster. The whole Polish economy was thus peculiarly susceptible, in the absence of insulating measures, to fluctuations in world trade in agricultural primary products.

Before we make an analysis of the economic problems of Polish agriculture, let us look first at the main outlines of its structure and organization. The basis of agriculture is of necessity the soil and its fertility. Although there is considerable va-

[1] See Table 5 on p. 25.

62

TABLE 20. POPULATION DEPENDENT ON AGRICULTURE (ABOUT 1930).*

Country and date	Population	Population dependent on agriculture	Per cent
	Thousands	*Thousands*	
Albania, 1930	1,003	800	80
Yugoslavia, 1931	13,934	10,629	76
Bulgaria, 1926	5,479	4,088	75
Rumania, 1930	18,057	13,069	72
Lithuania, c. 1930	2,367	1,657	70
Poland, 1931	32,107	19,347	60
Finland, 1930	3,562	2,015	57
Estonia, 1934	1,126	626	56
Latvia, 1930	1,900	1,036	55
Ireland, 1926	2,972	1,561	53
Hungary, 1930	8,688	4,472	51
Spain, 1930	23,564	11,864	50
Portugal, 1930	6,360	2,954	46
Greece, 1928	6,205	2,829	46
Italy, 1931	41,177	17,953	44
Czechoslovakia, 1930	14,730	4,812	33
Sweden, 1930	6,142	1,906	31
Denmark, 1930	3,551	1,061	30
Northern Ireland, 1926	1,257	372	30
France, 1931	41,228	11,890	29
Luxembourg, c. 1930	300	85	28
Norway, 1930	2,814	762	27
Austria, 1934	6,760	1,772	26
Switzerland, 1930	4,066	901	22
Germany, 1933	66,029	13,297	20
Netherlands, 1930	7,936	1,436	18
Belgium, 1930	8,092	1,190	15
Scotland, 1931	4,843	387	8
England and Wales, 1931	39,952	2,117	5

* *Source: Economic Demography of Eastern and Southern Europe* (Geneva: League of Nations, 1945), p. 26, table 2.

riety in the types of soil found in Poland owing to the alternation of clays and sands which have resulted from glacial conditions in prehistoric times, it is a not too inaccurate generalization to say that the soils, particularly in the northern and central lowlands, are podsols associated with temperate forest regions. This type of soil, which lacks phosphates and calcium, requires careful cultivation and the skillful use of fertilizers if it is to produce adequate yields. These conditions were mainly satisfied in western Poland and parts of central Poland. Although the soils in these areas were of only medium fertility, the higher standards of cultivation, including the intelligent use of fertilizers, made these areas the best developed agriculturally. It was an unfortunate fact that the area of densest agricultural population—southeastern Poland—was also the most relatively backward area from the technical agricultural point of view. It is important to remember that there were huge differences in agricultural output between the western and the eastern provinces of Poland. Indeed, we may say that the difference between the western and the eastern provinces was equal to that between countries of highly developed agriculture and those of backward and primitive agriculture.

A marked feature of Polish agriculture was that in spite of an important trend toward mixed farming, crop production predominated over livestock production. In the years before the war of 1939 to 1945, there were, however, important developments in the rearing of livestock, especially of pigs, and in the creation of new lines of export, such as bacon and tinned ham, dependent on the rearing of livestock. The latest available data of the utilization of land in Poland are set out in Table 21.

Examining the area sown and the yield per hectare, we find that the principal field crops were rye, potatoes, oats, wheat, barley, and beets. Details are set out in Table 22.

In the period 1934 to 1938, it will be seen that, according

TABLE 21. UTILIZATION OF LAND IN POLAND (1931).*

	Thousand hectares	Percentage of total area
Total area of Poland	38,005	100.0
Total used for agriculture	25,661	67.5
Arable	18,607	49.0
Orchards, market gardens	554	1.5
Meadows	3,808	10.0
Pasture	2,692	7.0
Forest	8,351	22.0
Other	3,993	10.5

* *Source:* Based on *Concise Statistical Year-Book of Poland, 1939–41,* p. 33, table 5.

TABLE 22. PRINCIPAL FIELD CROPS OF POLAND; ANNUAL MEAN FIGURES FOR FOUR PERIODS.*

Years	Rye	Potatoes	Oats	Wheat	Barley	Beets
(Area sown in thousand hectares)						
1909–1913	5,087	2,404	2,749	1,353	1,265	168
1924–1928	5,552	2,423	1,978	1,307	1,118	195
1929–1933	5,777	2,696	2,195	1,662	1,228	158
1934–1938	5,774	2,900	2,250	1,738	1,199	130

Years	Beets	Potatoes	Wheat	Barley	Oats	Rye
(Yield per hectare in quintals)						
1909–1913	245	103	12.4	11.8	10.2	11.2
1924–1928	200	102	11.4	11.2	10.3	10.0
1929–1933	212	113	11.8	12.1	11.6	11.4
1934–1938	216	121	11.9	11.8	11.4	11.2

* *Source: Concise Statistical Year-Book of Poland, 1939–41,* p. 35, table 8.

to the area sown, the order of importance of the principal field crops was rye, potatoes, oats, wheat, barley, beets. In the same period, the order of importance by yields per unit of area was beets, potatoes, wheat, barley, oats, and rye. Taken by all criteria, however, rye was the main agricultural product, followed by potatoes. Then came oats, wheat, barley, and beets. This last crop was the most profitable. If we look at agricultural output in relation to that of other European countries, we find that Poland came second only to Germany in the production of potatoes and rye, third after Germany and France for oats, fourth for barley after Germany, Rumania, and Spain, fourth also for beets after Germany, Czechoslovakia, and France, and seventh for wheat. During the period of the world economic crisis there was a great increase in potato production, for the peasant on his small holding could grow enough potatoes to keep himself and his family alive on a self-subsistence basis, but he could not do this if he cultivated rye or wheat. The world economic crisis in point of fact brought to Poland the worst agricultural crisis in eighty years.

When we turn to consideration of livestock production we find that the order of importance was cattle, pigs, horses, sheep, and goats. Detailed statistics are given in Table 23. The figures of this table assume more significance when we compare them with the corresponding figures for other countries as is done in Table 24.

A minor branch of agriculture, if it can so be classified, which should not be overlooked, was the cultivation of fresh-water fish in the fishponds which covered many thousands of acres in Poland. Carp was the principal fish for this purpose, and in 1938 the annual "production" of carp in Poland was about 12,000 tons, while 14,000 tons of carp and pike were taken from the lakes.

In this period, and particularly from 1929 to 1938, the Polish sea fisheries also made great strides, not only in absolute figures

TABLE 23. LIVESTOCK IN POLAND (IN THOUSAND HEAD)
(1930–1938).*

Year	Cattle	Pigs	Horses	Sheep	Goats
1930	9,399	6,047	4,103	2,492	227
1931	9,785	7,321	4,124	2,599	237
1932	9,461	5,844	3,940	2,488	248
1933	8,985	5,753	3,773	2,557	278
1934	9,258	4,091	3,764	2,554	321
1935	9,759	6,723	3,760	2,802	355
1936	10,200	7,060	3,824	3,024	383
1937	10,572	7,696	3,890	3,188	406
1938	10,554	7,525	3,916	3,411	420

* Source: Based on Concise Statistical Year-Book of Poland, 1939–41, p. 39, table 17.

TABLE 24. LIVESTOCK IN CERTAIN SELECTED COUNTRIES (IN THOUSAND
HEAD) (1937/1938).*

Year	Country	Cattle	Pigs	Horses	Sheep
1938	Poland	10,554	7,525	3,916	3,411
1937	Canada	8,841	3,093	2,883	3,340
1937	Czechoslovakia	4,930	3,611	704	624
1938	Denmark	3,183	2,845	564	187
1938	France	15,662	7,127	2,692	9,872
1938	Germany	19,911	23,481	3,443	4,809
1938	Hungary	1,750	3,110	814	1,629
1938	Great Britain	8,697	4,366	1,096	26,302
1938	U.S.A.	66,821	49,011	10,800	53,762
1938	U.S.S.R.	63,200	30,600	17,500	102,500
1937	Yugoslavia	4,169	3,180	1,249	9,909

* Source: Based on Concise Statistical Year-Book of Poland, 1939–41, p. 40, table 19.

but relatively in the size and value of the average catch per fisherman. Details are set out in Table 25.

TABLE 25. DEVELOPMENT OF POLISH SEA FISHERIES (1929–1938).*

Year	Number of fishermen	Total catch	Annual catch per man		Total catch
		Thousand quintals	*Quintals*	*Thousand zloty*	*Thousand zloty*
1929	1,370	27.8	20.3	2.6	3,630.0
1931	1,587	57.7	36.1	1.5	2,393.7
1933	1,631	139.6	85.6	2.8	4,589.4
1934	1,687	145.0	86.0	2.4	3,991.8
1935	1,730	171.1	98.9	2.0	3,431.7
1936	1,780	233.2	131.0	2.2	3,986.0
1937	1,822	140.1	76.9	2.8	5,127.3
1938	1,955	125.2	64.0	3.7	7,181.7

* *Source:* Based on *Concise Statistical Year-Book of Poland, 1939–41*, p. 40, table 20.

With some 22 per cent of the country covered by forest, the timber resources of Poland and their utilization naturally formed an important branch of agriculture. Unfortunately, they suffered from excessive and often reckless cutting. The excessive exploitation may be seen from the following figures: before 1939 Polish lumber amounted to 6 per cent of the entire annual production of Europe, while the forest surface of Poland amounted to only 3 per cent of the European forest surface. Or, if we consider world figures, Polish lumber amounted to 2 per cent of world production, but the Polish forest surface was only 0.3 per cent of the world forest surface.

Although it is dangerous to make generalizations about standards of living in a country where there are such marked regional differences as those between western and eastern Poland, it is fair to say that the representative inhabitant of the rural areas was the poor peasant with insufficient resources to keep himself and his family in any kind of decency according to western European, let alone American, standards. This was true even in the period before the world economic depression, but the position became much worse in consequence of that depression. It is notoriously difficult to make, for comparative purposes, any accurate computation of the income of the independent peasant farmer (the class which in Poland made up the greater part of the rural population). We can, however, make some fairly reasonable estimates. The actual distribution of the agrarian population according to the 1921 census was: independent peasants, 70.5 per cent; landless peasants, 15.0 per cent; and hired workers, 14.5 per cent. Although the relative proportions of these figures may have changed somewhat over the period to 1939, they remained sufficiently constant to indicate the general position. Of the great mass of independent peasants, we can say only that they lived at an exceedingly low level. It has been estimated, for example, that agricultural earnings in western Europe were normally three times as high as the level of peasant earnings in Poland. For the most part, the Polish peasants were self-sufficient in foodstuffs. Sometimes and in some places, however—notably Polesie—the peasants lived below any reasonable subsistence level, and always and in all places they had such a low purchasing power that their poverty stood in the way of the development of the internal market of the country. There was thus a failure to give adequate stimulus to the industrialization which alone could solve the problems of rural overpopulation and of "concealed unemployment." Before we go on to discuss these problems, however, it is worth while to look at the wage statistics for daily farm laborers.

Table 26 must be used with care in making deductions about the general earnings of the Polish peasants, since it gives the *wages* of the smallest sector of the peasantry, and it must be remembered that in an agricultural country wages are by no means the same as earnings. The hired worker may, for instance, have a cow and an allotment of his own which would increase his "real earnings" but which would not be shown in the wage

69

TABLE 26. WAGES OF DAILY FARM LABORERS (DAILY WAGES IN ZLOTY) (1928 AND 1933).*

Description	Work people on own board		Work people boarded by employer	
	1928	1933	1928	1933
Spring season				
Man	3.9	1.7	2.7	1.3
Woman	2.6	1.3	1.8	1.0
Juvenile	2.4	1.1	1.6	0.8
Man and pair of horses	16.9	8.3	12.6	6.7
Summer season				
Man	5.6	2.5	4.1	1.9
Woman	3.5	1.9	2.5	1.4
Juvenile	2.9	1.5	2.0	1.2
Man and pair of horses	17.3	8.5	13.3	6.9
Autumn season				
Man	3.9	1.6	2.8	1.3
Woman	2.9	1.3	2.1	1.1
Juvenile	2.4	1.0	1.7	0.9
Man and pair of horses	16.3	7.3	12.6	5.7

* Source: Concise Statistical Year-Book of Poland, 1939–41, p. 116, table 12.

statistics. Certain allowances should also be made on account of food and accommodation supplied him. We must remember, however, that the national income per head of Poland in 1929 was far lower than the corresponding figure for such countries as Great Britain or France and was higher than only such low-standard countries as Bulgaria or Greece. When we bear this fact in mind, it is reasonable to assume that the independent peasant was not much better off than the farm laborer working for wages. The earnings of the independent peasant, it is safe to assume, would follow the same trends as those of the farm laborer, and it is in this connection that Table 26 is mainly valuable, for it shows in striking fashion the severity of the impact of the economic depression between 1928 and 1933 upon peasant earnings. This phenomenon is also well brought out by Table 27.

TABLE 27. INDEX NUMBERS OF THE ANNUAL WAGES OF POLISH
AGRICULTURAL WORKERS (1928/1929 TO 1937/1938).*

1928–1929	100	1931–1932	61
1929–1930	69	1932–1933	47
1930–1931	54	1937–1938	53

* Source: George Kagan, "Agrarian Régime of Pre-War Poland," *Journal of Central European Affairs*, Oct., 1943, p. 241.

What this sudden change meant in human terms can be understood from such descriptions of living conditions in rural areas as the following:

We eat potatoes three times a day, potatoes, of course, without any seasoning. We are crawling with lice because we cannot afford soap. . . . A slice of bread is only for a big occasion. [Radomsk district, voivodship of Lodz.]

We use no sugar, save for big holidays, and we forego even salt, as it is expensive. . . . The labourer raises pigs, chickens, and then sells them for almost nothing, as he is obliged to sell them and cannot enjoy eating them. He lives mostly on potatoes, cabbage, bread and milk in summer; in winter he lacks milk. [Lancut district, voivodship of Lwów.]

The floors in the stables and pigsties are ruined, and the farmer cannot afford to repair them. . . . He cannot afford to buy planks or nails for they are expensive. . . . The hut is made of mud, and has no floor. . . . The stables are no better, and the barns often have no

71

walls. The dog has no shelter and we pity him. . . . One bucket for the whole household and land holding. This bucket serves to carry water to the kitchen, to feed the horse, the cow, and the pig, to draw water from the well. The wagon and the plough are rotting in the rain for there is no shelter for them and one cannot build for lack of means. [Buczacz district, voivodship of Tarnopo.]

It should be remembered that these descriptions, taken from the *Peasants' Memoirs* published in 1935 by the Polish Institute of Social Economy, are of conditions immediately after the impact of a devastatingly severe agricultural crisis. Conditions began to improve considerably after 1936.

The root cause of this desperate poverty was that the Polish peasant, especially in the south, suffered from a shortage of land. Taken in conjunction with the low level of agricultural technique, the high birth rate and the restrictions on immigration into the United States, Brazil, and Canada (countries which before 1914 had absorbed a steady stream of Polish emigrants), the problem of rural overpopulation was indeed a formidable one. The solution adopted was a double one—the redistribution of the land to create economically sound holdings and at the same time the absorption into industry of the rural proletariat left unemployable in agriculture. The solution of the problem of rural overpopulation was thus integrally connected with the problem of the industrial development of the country. The surplus population provided a labor force available for new industries, and at the same time its removal from agriculture raised the standard of living of those remaining and thus assisted in creating an internal market for the products of the new industries, quite apart from any market provided by the industrial workers themselves.

The redistribution of the land was necessary to correct the economic distortions which flowed from two extremes: at the one limit were the great latifundia, at the other were small plots quite incapable of supporting in any decency even one farmer and his family. We can obtain an accurate picture from the statistics in Table 28.

TABLE 28. DISTRIBUTION OF POLISH LANDHOLDINGS (1931).*

Area (hectares)	Number of holdings	Per cent
Under 2	747,100	25.5
2–5	1,136,100	38.7
5–10	728,700	24.8
10–15	190,900	6.5
15–50	118,200	4.0
50 and over	14,700	0.5
Total	2,935,700	100.0

* *Source:* Based on *Concise Statistical Year-Book of Poland, 1939–41,* p. 31, table 1.

There were also tiresome survivals of feudal rights, and in addition there was much waste land capable of reclamation. Agricultural reform thus took four forms:

(1) Parcellation of excessively large estates

(2) Commassation, i.e., the bringing together of excessively small strips in order to make an economically viable unit

(3) Paying off rights of common, which had contributed greatly to sowing discord between the estate owners and the peasantry

(4) Various measures of land amelioration, including the reclamation of waste land.

One of the first acts of the new republic was the passing of the Agrarian Reform Act of 1920. There was a rapid rise in demand for land on the part of small farmers, who were quick to profit from the famine conditions of the towns, and also in the supply of land by the large owners, who were threatened by compulsory expropriation. After 1921, the peasantry became impoverished, and the act was not effectively enforced, so that in the next few years sales and purchases of land fell rapidly. In

73

1925 the passing of an additional land reform act gave a fresh stimulus to the redistribution of land, and for a few years there was a rapid growth in the numbers of peasant proprietors. Moreover, in order to speed the process, credit facilities were offered to peasant buyers by the government. The movement was rapidly getting under way when it received a severe check in consequence of the onset of the world economic depression. For a time, the low level of market prices for agricultural products caused the demand for land to drop almost to zero. From 1935 to the outbreak of war in 1939, however, there was a marked upward tendency once more, although the yearly figures fell short of those prevailing in 1926 to 1930. Detailed statistics for the period are set out in Table 29; they effectively refute the lie that land reform in Poland had to wait until the Soviet occupation.

In connection with parcellation, it must not be forgotten that as the large estates often obtained higher yields per hectare than the small ones, the breakup of the large estates meant a fall in yield per unit area. This loss was largely offset, however, by the gain in productive efficiency caused by the consolidation of small holdings. In point of fact, total production showed a substantial increase in spite of the fall in average yields of rye and wheat. Altogether some 6,300,000 acres were affected by the agrarian reforms, and well over 700,000 new model holdings were set up which afforded employment and livelihood to 3,500,000 peasants. The area of arable land increased by the reclamation of barren land was over 3,000,000 acres.

These were substantial achievements, but the problem of rural overpopulation and its accompanying "concealed unemployment" was far from being solved. For example, it was estimated in 1931 that in the district of Rzeszow of the 104,764 people working in agriculture 66,900 would be superfluous in a rationalized economy. In other words, 60 per cent of the active agricultural workers in that district could have left without

Table 29. Land Reform in Poland (1919–1938). *

Year	Parcellation		Commassation		Liquidation of easements			Melioration by regulation of rivers, drainage, etc.	
	Newly formed holdings	Area parceled	Holdings consolidated	Area consolidated	Holdings	Area exchanged for easements	Compensation paid	In thousand kilometers	On area
	Thousands	Thousand hectares	Thousands	Thousand hectares	Thousands	Thousand hectares	Thousand zloty		Thousand hectares
1919	2.1	11.8	2.5	19.2	0.1	0.3	—	—	—
1920	11.5	54.3	1.5	11.1	0.2	0.3	—	—	—
1921	29.7	180.4	2.3	18.5	1.4	4.8	—	—	—
1922	41.2	254.2	3.5	32.2	1.6	5.2	—	—	—
1923	43.5	201.7	5.2	39.2	2.1	5.5	—	—	—
1924	30.0	118.3	7.6	61.6	3.8	9.9	1.4	—	—
1925	28.6	128.3	8.6	75.5	7.3	16.8	2.6	—	—
1926	59.4	209.8	16.7	131.7	17.1	50.8	—	—	—
1927	67.0	245.1	29.6	237.0	27.0	85.8	3.0	—	0.5
1928	72.8	227.6	42.3	317.9	39.4	100.6	837.3	0.5	17.0
1929	55.9	164.5	56.5	416.5	34.0	94.4	762.3	1.2	29.4
1930	49.4	130.8	72.1	517.7	33.6	76.0	770.7	1.2	29.5
1931	36.4	105.3	76.8	565.5	32.7	45.8	487.8	1.3	43.4
1932	30.8	74.1	58.6	389.9	25.4	38.4	215.3	2.7	91.4
1933	28.7	83.5	61.8	392.3	12.1	16.9	352.0	1.9	66.1
1934	18.7	56.5	59.9	352.7	9.1	10.6	95.9	2.1	59.3
1935	24.5	49.8	83.3	473.4	10.0	10.5	110.4	2.2	58.9
1936	28.5	96.5	86.2	471.6	9.4	11.6	43.3	2.3	55.9
1937	37.7	113.1	93.7	470.2	6.6	4.7	114.2	3.6	97.3
1938	37.7	119.1	90.3	426.9	7.6	6.4	92.9	—	—
1919–38	734.1	2,654.8	859.0	5,423.3	280.5	595.3	889.1	19.0	548.7

* Source: Concise Statistical Year-Book of Poland, 1939–41, p. 32, table 4.

diminishing its output. For the country as a whole, there were various estimates made of the magnitude of this "concealed unemployment." They vary from 4,300,000 (Bicanic), which was probably too low, to 5,000,000 (Poniatowski) and even 8,455,000 (Oberlander), which was probably too high. No exact estimate can be made, but it is probably not too far wide of the mark to say that, even after the substantial measure of land reform achieved by 1938, there still remained a superfluous rural population of between five and six million.[2] Their removal would not have lowered output, given a reasonably efficient form of technical organization. As it was, they depressed the standard of living of the whole peasant economy and hindered the industrialization of the country.

The crux of the problem was that no mere change in the ownership of the land could have solved the agrarian problem of Poland. Given the agricultural technique of prewar Poland, there was a substantial part of the agricultural population which could not profitably be employed on the land. This economically surplus population, if it was to find employment, had to find it either through entry into industry or through the technical transformation of agriculture.

A League of Nations report, published in 1946, gives a much higher figure for "surplus" population than do any of the other authorities. These figures, which are based on computing a "standard" population, assuming French productivity per hectare of arable-equivalent agricultural land and French percapita level, and then deducting this "standard" population from the "actual" population, give the results for Poland shown in Table 30.

It is a very artificial calculation. The results, checked against those of other authorities, are far too high. If agricultural techniques were assumed to be improved, a much lower figure would

[2] These figures are given in George Kagan, "Agrarian Régime of Pre-War Poland," *Journal of Central European Affairs*, Oct., 1943.

TABLE 30. "SURPLUS" AGRICULTURAL POPULATION (ABOUT 1930).

Country and province *	Surplus population	
		Per cent
Poland	11,589,000	59.9
Central	4,389,000	59.4
East	2,339,000	53.6
South	4,220,000	71.6
West	640,000	37.5

* Source: *Economic Demography of Eastern and Southern Europe* (Geneva: League of Nations, 1945), p. 208.

be reached. Nevertheless, all calculations point to the conclusion that even with improved agrarian techniques, there was serious "concealed unemployment" in Polish agriculture. This state of affairs could be remedied only by industrialization as well as by agrarian reform and technical improvement. Agrarian reform, in short, was not so much a question of land reform in the distributist sense—though redistribution, parcellation, and commassation were essential preliminaries—as a question of creating new industries and at the same time of transforming the technique of Polish agriculture. Both these processes needed capital —and so we return once more to a root problem of the dynamics of the Polish economy in this period, the scarcity of capital.

So far as the application of increased capital to agriculture, in order to improve technique, cut costs, and thus eventually to raise profits, is concerned, there were unsuspected dangers. From 1926 to 1928, Polish peasants, so far as they were in a position to do so, invested substantially in fertilizers and in agricultural machinery, following a sensible policy of cutting technical costs in order to increase profits. Then came the world economic crisis and a catastrophic collapse of agricultural prices. The peasants found that they were saddled with onerous interest charges and mortgages, while their costs had not been cut

77

as low as the fall in prices had cut their gross income. By 1936, a medium-sized farm was worth less than half its 1929 price. The government helped deal with the situation by reducing interest rates and by declaring a form of debt moratorium, but its efforts in this direction did not go far enough to provide substantial relief on the scale required. In addition, the government granted credits for withholding crops from the market so that the peasants should not be compelled to sell their grain at distress prices during the most unfavorable season.

From 1928 onward, Poland developed substantial agricultural exports. They were encouraged by means of export premiums, while the domestic market was protected at the same time by heavy tariffs. During 1936 and 1937, after the bitter years of depression, there took place a remarkable recovery. This was the result not only of the rise in world agricultural prices but also of the internal industrial activity fostered by the government. Once again, we may note the close interconnection of industrialization and agricultural progress.

Developments which promised to be of great importance came late in 1938. In August, the government established a minimum price for rye at twenty zloty a quintal and also fixed the prices of other cereals proportionately. At the same time, the government attempted to raise the price of rye by export premiums, special credits, and the construction of grain elevators and other storage facilities. In November, a barter agreement was reached with Germany by which industrial machinery was to be exchanged against Polish cereals. The amount would have been in excess of normal exports to Germany. The effects of the increasingly unsettled international situation and finally of the outbreak of war in September, 1939, made it impossible to form any valid judgment on how these arrangements would have worked out.

78

CHAPTER 7

Industry

THROUGHOUT this period Poland had substantial domestic sources of industrial raw materials, although they were inadequate to meet fully the demands of Polish industry. A general impression of Polish mineral resources on the eve of World War II may be gathered from Table 31.

There were abundant supplies of coal, and the Silesian coalfield was of fundamental importance in the industrial development of the country. Its output was estimated potentially at about 60,000,000 tons a year. In 1929 actual production reached an output of 46,000,000 tons, and, although production declined in the years of depression, it showed a marked upward turn in the years immediately before the outbreak of war (Table 32). Actual output exceeded the industrial requirements of the country, and in point of fact coal proved one of the most important exports of Poland in this period, especially after 1926 when the Polish industry was not slow to take advantage of the opportunity presented by the British coal strike of 1926 in order to gain ground in markets hitherto dominated by British coal exports. Although the output of petroleum had steadily declined since the peak year of 1909, Polish output satisfied the country's needs. Shortly before the outbreak of war, however, the output of petroleum had declined to such an extent that it left no margin

TABLE 31. PRODUCTION OF MINING AND ALLIED INDUSTRIES (1938).*

Commodity	Production
	Thousand tons
Coal	38,100
Lignite	10
Iron ore	872
Zinc ore	498
Lead ore	44
Petroleum	507
Rock salt	643
Potassium salts	567
Pyrites	92
Phosphorites (1937)	15
Steel	1,441
Pig iron	879
Zinc	108
Lead	20
Sulphuric acid (1936)	137
Superphosphates (1935)	40
Cement (1936)	1,052
Coke	2,200
Cadmium (kg.)	265 (kg.)
Silver (kg.)	1,990 (kg.)
Natural gas (1937)	483,000 (000 cu.m.)

* *Source:* "Problems of Economic Geology in Poland" in *Polish Science and Learning,* no. 2, Feb., 1943.

for export, and if the process of industrialization had proceeded at its normal pace there would soon have developed a shortage which would have necessitated the import of petroleum or perhaps of crude oil (since the working capacity of the oil refineries exceeded actual output) or developing substitutes. Lead, zinc, and silver had been extracted in the Silesian area since mediaeval times, and the zinc deposits were particularly important.

Exports of zinc to Germany and Czechoslovakia were considerable in the years before 1939. The amount of lead produced, however, was not sufficient for Poland's own requirements. The iron ore found in Poland was of low quality and, again, the total production was not sufficient for Polish requirements. Poland was fortunate in possessing vast deposits of salt, which were of fundamental importance in the development of Poland's chemical industries. In addition, there were considerable deposits of the rarer potassium salts, important in the preparation of artificial fertilizers.

TABLE 32. MINERAL OUTPUT OF POLAND IN THOUSAND TONS (1913–1938).*

Year	Coal (million tons)	Crude petro- leum	Salt	Potas- sium salts	Iron ore	Lead ore	Zinc ore
1913	41.0	1,114	—	14	493	502	57.0
1928	40.6	743	548	342	699	321	17.0
1932	28.8	557	492	299	77	43	5.5
1936	29.7	511	552	434	468	143	5.9
1937	36.2	501	590	521	792	191	8.9
1938	38.1	507	643	567	872	498	44.0

* Source: Extracted from Concise Statistical Year-Book of Poland, 1939–41, p. 53, table 9.

Poland had, however, no manganese, nickel, copper, tin, aluminum, rubber or cotton. Wool was available only in small quantities. The result was that in the years immediately before the war, half of Polish imports were made up of industrial raw materials—a situation which threw great strain on Poland's balance of trade—and as industrialization proceeded the problem of the importation of the necessary raw materials became one of increasing difficulty.

Before 1914, apart from the Galician oil field, Silesia, and the

Lodz industrial district, there were virtually no industrial areas in Poland—only a scattering of factories here and there throughout the country. The Old Polish Mining Basin, made up of the Kielce region, the Lublin plateau, and the Sandomierz plain, had been an important industrial region in the sixteenth century. At that period, it had had iron smelting works and foundries, glass and pottery works, a textile industry, and a copper smelting industry. Jan Malachowski had ordered blast furnaces to be built at Staporkow in 1739, Ruski Brod in 1750, and Janow in 1755. If Poland had not been partitioned by Russia, Prussia, and Austria, these works might have provided the nucleus of a heavy industry and a foundation for a Polish industrial revolution. The Polish government at the time of the Duchy of Warsaw and of the Congress Kingdom had attempted to develop industries, but these beginnings were deliberately cut short by the policies of the partitioning powers. Every part of Poland was frontier territory to one of the partitioning powers and was thus regarded as territory in which, for military reasons, as little vital industry as possible should be located. The two exceptions to this general policy of economic barrenness were the Galician oil industry and the textile industries centered around Lodz, which had the advantage of access to the vast market of Russia and which were also protected from foreign competition by a high tariff wall.

Such industrial establishments, however, as had existed before 1914 were largely destroyed during the course of hostilities. Not only was Poland turned into a battlefield for almost six years, but the Germans pursued a policy of the deliberate destruction of industrial plants in order to obtain raw materials for their own war machine and at the same time in order to achieve the destruction of a potential competitor to their own industries in the postwar markets of east-central and eastern Europe. In Lodz alone, for example, the Germans seized more than 1,000 electric motors, over 1,000 tons of copper, broken from machines, and 1,300 kilometers of leather transmission belting. Thus, so far as industrial equipment was concerned, the restored Poland had to start virtually from scratch.

By 1939, however, Poland had become a moderately industrialized country with 20 per cent of the population deriving its livelihood from industry. (Comparative figures were 38 per cent for Germany and 11 per cent for Yugoslavia.) There was a marked divergence in degree of industrialization, however, between the area west of the Vistula, containing the great industrial centers of Silesia, Czestochowa, Lodz, and Warsaw, and the area east of the Vistula. It was in part to correct this undesirable distribution of industry that plans were made for developing the Central Industrial District, an area embracing the greater part of the triangle limited by Warsaw, Cracow, and Lwów.

The main course of development of the principal Polish industries after 1919 was in the following pattern: an unstable period during the postwar inflation, a setback as a result of the deflationary effects of Grabski's financial reforms, a steady upward movement on a firm economic foundation from 1927 to 1929, then a second severe setback caused by the impact of the world economic crisis on the Polish economy and prolonged by the government's determination to maintain the exchange value of the zloty, and finally marked recovery and a steady upward movement after 1936. If we arrange the main Polish industries in their order of importance as measured by the numbers of workers employed, we find the pattern set out in Table 33.

Pride of place was thus accorded to the textile industries, which went back in their origin to the policy of the Congress Kingdom (1815 to 1830) in encouraging the immigration of Czech, Saxon, and other foreign artisans to lay the foundations of Polish industry. At the beginning of the nineteenth century, Lodz was an insignificant village. There was a good water supply. The locality was government property so that industrialists were able to obtain sites on favorable terms. There was a ready supply of cheap labor. Behind a high tariff wall, the industry

TABLE 33. PRINCIPAL POLISH INDUSTRIES ACCORDING TO NUMBER OF WORKERS (1937).*

Industry	Workers employed
Textiles	157,100
Metal manufactures	155,700
Mining	98,800
Foodstuffs	86,500
Stone, glass, and ceramics	81,000
Timber	68,100
Chemical	54,600
Building	50,300
Electrotechnical	17,500
Paper	17,300
Clothing	17,100
Printing and allied trades	14,100
Leather	10,400
Toys	400
Total: Industry alone	730,100
Total: Industry and mining	828,900

* Source: Extracted from Concise Statistical Year-Book of Poland, 1939–41, p. 50, table 1.

could concentrate on producing the cheapest type of textiles to cater to the needs of eastern Europe and Asiatic Russia. The result was that Lodz surged ahead until it became the "Manchester of Poland" with a population of 673,000 in 1938, of whom 111,772 were workers employed in the 2,092 industrial enterprises of the district. Of the various textiles, cotton easily ranked first and was followed at some distance by wool. Silk was of little importance, since it was a new line which was only beginning to develop in the years immediately before the outbreak of war in 1939. Apart from Lodz, Bialystok, and Bielsko were the other main centers of the textile industries. Each of these main centers had its own specialty: Lodz produced cotton goods, woolen rugs, haberdashery, natural and artificial silk, laces, curtains and embroideries. Bialystok specialized in woolen rugs, haberdashery, and garments. Bielsko specialized in high-quality woolen fabrics.

The metal industries of Poland were varied in their products as may be seen from Table 34.

TABLE 34. PRODUCTION OF THE POLISH METAL INDUSTRIES (1936).*

Product	Tons
Steel	1,145,000
Rolled iron	826,000
Pig iron	584,000
Iron wire nails	30,700
Drawn iron wire	27,300
Galvanized iron sheets	26,400

* Source: Extracted from Concise Statistical Year-Book of Poland, 1939–41, p. 53, table 9; p. 55, table 13.

In addition to the items listed above, other products of the metal industries were metal bedsteads, railway cars, locomotives, steam boilers, internal combustion engines, pumps, woodworking and metalworking machinery, agricultural and textile machinery, and electrical apparatus of various kinds. The Polish metal industries had a history going back to the period of partition when, even after Russia had begun to develop her own industries, iron bridges, boilers, motors, and agricultural machinery were supplied throughout the Russian Empire by Polish firms in Warsaw, Sosnowiec, and Lublin. The war of 1914 hit the Polish industries very hard, for much of the industrial plant was confiscated and removed to Russia or Germany. Throughout the period from 1919 to 1939 there was steady and substantial development, but the possibilities which still remained even at the end of the period for further expansion in the internal market alone may be estimated from a comparison of the consumption of iron per head per year in western and in eastern Poland: Silesia, 63 kilograms; E. Provinces 1.41 kilograms.

In the mining industries, coal easily took first place. The order of importance of the various mining industries, ranged according to output, is given in Table 35.

TABLE 35. THE MINING INDUSTRIES OF POLAND (1936).*

Product	Output
	Tons
Coal	29,747,000
Oil	511,000
Rock and brine salt	467,000
Potassium salts	434,000
Iron ore	469,000
Zinc ore	143,000
Lead ore	6,000

* Source: Extracted from *Concise Statistical Year-Book of Poland, 1939–41*, p. 53, table 9.

Among world exporters of coal, Poland stood seventh in 1936 and was third among European exporters. The high-quality technical equipment and organization which were characteristic of the Silesian industry before 1914 were maintained under Polish management throughout the period.

The foodstuffs industry covered a miscellany of products. Pride of place was taken by the beet sugar industry which in 1936 produced 4.5 million quintals of raw sugar and exported over 62,000 tons of refined sugar. The export of processed foods such as canned ham, meat, fish, and vegetables was also developing rapidly in the years immediately before 1939.

The stone, glass, and ceramics industries took something like ten years to get back to their prewar level of production. More-over, demand lagged behind the development of productive capacity. Nevertheless, shortly before the outbreak of war in 1939, Polish glassware was exported to fifty-five countries. Annual production in this group of industries amounted to 80,000 tons of glass, 842,600 tons of cement, 556,750 tons of lime, 42,000 tons of glass hollow ware, 26,000 tons of plate glass, 11,570 tons of faïence, 4,020 tons of china, over 1,300 million bricks, and 43 million tiles.

The timber industries included not only the production of timber proper, but also such allied industries as the making of furniture (centered largely in Bydgoszcz), the making of matches, and paper making. The importance of Polish timber may be seen from Table 36.

TABLE 36. EXPORTS OF POLISH TIMBER (1936).

Type	Tons
Sawed wood	952,740
Round wood	275,005
Sleepers	123,225
Pulpwood	123,084
Plywood	54,267
Pit props	30,047
Tele-technical poles	13,161
Not classified	107,046
Total	1,678,575

The Poles showed something akin to genius in their develop-ment of chemical industries, particularly in the production of artificial fertilizers, a key industry in a predominantly agricul-tural country. Professor Moscicki, who became president of the republic in 1926, originally made his reputation by his man-agement of the Chorzow nitrate factory, one of the largest chemi-cal factories in Europe. The Chorzow factory was a powerful link between agriculture and industry. Its success led to the founding by the state of a second factory at Tarnow. In addition to fertilizers, the Polish chemical industries produced coal derivatives, dyestuffs, artificial fibers, oil, soap, scent, paint and lacquer, explosives, celluloid, plastics, and rubber goods. Warsaw in particular had a very good reputation for the production of perfumes and cosmetics. Exports included artificial fertilizers, artificial silk, superphosphates, benzol, zinc white, tar, carbide, soda ash, ammonium sulphate, oil cakes, explosives, oilcloth, glue, potassium carbonate, and ammonium chloride and carbonate.

As a consequence of the wholesale destruction of buildings throughout the war years, especially in the eastern provinces, Poland started her new existence in 1919 with an acute housing shortage. The building industry, however, was sluggish in meeting the demand. The main reason for this was lack of capital. So far as state capital was concerned, funds were wanted for more urgent purposes. Nevertheless, such aid as was possible was given. Provincial and municipal authorities could do little, though the record of the city of Warsaw in the years before the war was very good. The main source of funds was the credits granted by the Bank of National Economy. Private building, however, remained one of the sectors of Polish industry which lagged behind the level of general development.

The development of the electrical industries also lagged behind hopes; for example, President Narutowicz's dream of hydroelectric production utilizing the fall of the rivers on the northern slopes of the Carpathians remained unfulfilled because of lack of capital. The law of 1922 regulating the conditions of the production and distribution of electricity paved the way for a rational development which aimed at concentrating production on large stations rather than at allowing the unchecked growth of uneconomic small stations. Nevertheless, the production of electricity remained at a comparatively low level. The production of electrical machinery and apparatus, however, was on a higher level.

Like the textile industries, the clothing industries date back to the period of partition. In Russian Poland, the clothing industry was principally a domestic industry. After the war, however, the huge demand for clothing gave rise to a sudden uprush of shoe, clothing, linen, and hat factories. Although the shoe industry of Czechoslovakia and the linen industry of Czechoslovakia and Austria made their competition felt in Poland, nevertheless Polish exports of shoes and ready-made clothing showed signs of developing significantly.

As might have been expected in a new state, demands on the printing industry were very great, from the production of paper money through the usual range of government publications to schoolbooks to replace the German and Russian textbooks previously used. Apart from the volume of production, the Polish printing industry could claim a remarkably high level of technical achievement, as in the maps and atlases produced by the firm of "Ksiaznica Atlas" under the superintendence of Professor Romer or the illustrated books produced by Jacob Mortkowicz.

Mention must also be made of the leather industry. Before 1914, the tanneries of Russian Poland produced mainly coarse-quality articles in the mass. The industry was practically ruined by the war, but this phase enabled a new beginning to be made and developments after 1919 were in the direction of raising quality rather than of increasing mass production. The industry was severely affected by the various crises, however, particularly since it was dependent on the importation of certain types of hide (for example, South American hides for soles) for uses for which the hides of Polish cattle were unfitted.

The main influence in shaping the structure of Polish industry as a whole during the period from 1919 to 1939 was the lack of capital combined with a situation which demanded both extensive and intensive investment in fixed capital. It became clear that this situation could be met satisfactorily in a relatively undeveloped and economically backward country only by planned industrial development. This solution, however, did not mean the abandonment of private enterprise, although more and more it was found necessary to bring private enterprise under state control. The general lines of state economic policy adopted in this field took the following pattern:

(1) The maintenance of equilibrium between state revenue and state expenditure, in order to avoid the draining off of capital accumulation from industrial investment;

(2) A steady development of public works;

(3) Strict control of the money market;

(4) The provision of incentives to private enterprise.

State investments, particularly after the rise to power in Germany of Hitler, had two main aims: the strengthening of the defensive potential of the country by developing a native armaments industry, and the provision of works which would make possible the further development of private industry and thus have a "multiplier" effect; for example, schemes of electrification and the improvement of communications. The best illustration of this process actually at work was the development of the Central Industrial District which is described later in this chapter.

In the twenty years of independence, annual investment in industrial developments amounted approximately to 5 per cent of the national income, or eighteen billion (milliard) zloty in 1938. What this meant in terms of actual industrial development may be judged from one or two examples. Between 1921 and 1931 (two censual years), the percentage of people employed in mining and industry increased by 25 per cent. In 1929, 68 per cent of the total value of Polish production was accounted for by agriculture and only 32 per cent by mining and industry. By 1939, mining and industry accounted for over 50 per cent of the value of the total production of the country. If it is argued

that value figures for 1929 and for 1939 are not strictly compa-
rable for this purpose, owing to the relatively greater fall in the
prices of agricultural produce as against those of industrial
products we can use changes in the general index of industrial
production as our criterion. The conclusion remains unchanged:
the Polish government's policy of industrialization had been
successful.

TABLE 37. INDEX OF POLISH INDUSTRIAL PRODUCTION (1922–1939).*

1928 = 100	
Year	Index
1922–27	45.5
1928	100.0
1932	64.0
1933	70.0
1934	79.0
1935	85.0
1936	94.0
1937	111.0
1938	119.0
1939 (spring)	125.8

* Source: Based primarily on Concise Statistical Year-Book of Poland,
1939–41, p. 67, table 24.

If we exclude the U.S.S.R., we may say that state capitalism
was developed in Poland to a greater extent than in any other
European country during this period. Exclusive of the armed
forces, the Polish government in 1939 had in its employ about
one million people and owned and controlled property valued
at some 4,000 million zloty. This total included about 100 industrial enterprises made up of more than 1,000 establishments,
which included the most important industries in the country.
The armaments industry was entirely state-owned; 80 per cent
of the chemical industry, 40 per cent of the iron industry, and

50 per cent of the remaining metallurgical industries were in the hands of the state. In addition, the state owned the entire commercial aviation (the Polish airlines, "Lot"), 95 per cent of the mercantile marine, and 93 per cent of the railways. The state also owned the largest forests in central Europe, which covered an area of over 3,000,000 hectares (of which over 2,-600,000 hectares formed a producing area), and was the owner and manager of five monopolies: alcohol, matches, tobacco, salt, and a state lottery. Reference has already been made in Chapter 5 to the state's interests in banking and credit, which should be used to supplement this account to give a total picture of the state's intervention in economic matters. It may be estimated that in 1932/1933, state enterprises in Poland had a turnover of about 17 per cent of the general turnover of industry and commerce. The percentage increased considerably between 1932 and 1939 in consequence of the development of the central industrial region. In the years immediately before the outbreak of war, something like one-third of the government's revenue came from state enterprises and monopolies.

Apart from the importance of state capitalism in the structure of Polish industry during this period, the other striking organizational feature was the dominant part played by cartels.[1] In fact, it is not going too far if we say that, with the exception of textiles, every important Polish industry was organized into a cartel. The importance of this factor may be judged when we mention that in 1930 some 56 cartels controlled approximately 37 per cent of the total industrial production of the country. The effects of the world economic depression on the Polish economy led among other things to an increased tendency toward cartellization, as might have been expected, for the cartels' policy of agreeing to quotas of production, fixing prices, and maintaining

[1] For an excellent factual account of Polish cartels, see R. L. Buell, *Poland: Key to Europe* (London, 1939), pp. 169 ff.

prices in the home market while "dumping" abroad at uneconomic prices was calculated to maximize profits and to lessen
the possibility of losses on a depressed market. The tendency
toward increasing cartellization was, of course, encouraged by
the Polish policy of a high protective tariff.

It would be erroneous, however, to give the impression that
the cartels were purely predatory in character and operations or
that the consumer was left unprotected against their extortions.
In defense of some of the cartels, it may be argued that since
costs of production in the same industry varied greatly in different parts of Poland, a legacy of the economic division of the
country under the rule of the partitioning powers, if the normal
working of the laws of supply and demand had been allowed to
operate, the high-cost enterprises would have been driven out
of existence and production would have been concentrated on
the low-cost plants. In a model economy and in the long run, it
might be said that this process should have been allowed to take
place. In the actual world, Poland could not ignore the short-
term fact that much invested capital would have been rendered
worthless and that many thousands of workers would have become unemployed. In a country such as Poland from 1919 to
1939, where the major economic problem around which the
working of the whole economy turned was a dearth of capital
and great "concealed unemployment," short-term interests in-
evitably had to carry greater weight in the formulation of policy
than long-term and somewhat unrealistic concepts of ideal maximum economic efficiency. Competition could not be allowed to
operate freely in such a manner as to destroy existing plant, even
if it were relatively inefficient. Hence, so far as a policy of
cartellization kept industrial plant in operation which otherwise would have been driven out of existence, a strong defense
can be made out for it on the grounds that it conserved capital
in a country which was desperately short of capital and that it

93

maintained industrial employment in a country where the need for maintaining and increasing industrial as against agricultural employment was of primary importance.

It may be argued, however, that by maintaining prices in the home market and so leading to a reduction in consumption, the cartels' policy caused more unemployment indirectly than it created employment directly and that cartels thus depressed the standard of living in this indirect way. The first point in this counterargument is very largely a matter of opinion and can neither be proved nor disproved. The theoretical solution to the problem is indeterminate. Evidence of the facts necessary to a solution is lacking, so it must be left open to individual interpretations. On the second point, however, there is ample factual evidence to show that the interests of consumers were not left to the unregulated mercy of cartel policy. The state intervened with no little success to protect the consumer by interpreting the meaning of the "public interest" under the Cartel Law as being the equivalent of the maintenance of "economically justifiable" prices.

The activities of cartels were regulated under the Cartel Law of March 28, 1933, modified by the presidential decree of November 27, 1935. The actual execution of detailed control was through the instrument of the cartel register of the Ministry of Commerce and Industry. There were three main means of control:

(1) All cartel agreements had to be registered within 14 days of their conclusion under a penalty of 50,000 zloty for noncompliance

(2) Officials of the Ministry of Commerce and Industry could inspect all the books and records of cartels

(3) The Minister of Commerce and Industry could under certain conditions dissolve a cartel.

The powers of the minister in this latter respect and the grounds for exercising them were clearly set out in the Cartel Law, which laid it down that if the minister believed that a cartel agreement or its administration was harmful to the public interest, or if he considered that the regulation of production and prices was economically unjustifiable, then he could dissolve the cartel either totally or partially and could free the members from the obligations which they had assumed in the cartel agreement. The cartel had the right of appeal to the Cartel Court, which was made up of three judges of the Supreme Court, one representative of the government, and one Chamber of Commerce expert in industrial and economic problems. Decisions of the Cartel Court were final and without appeal.

That these legal safeguards for the consumer were not merely paper protection was seen in the years from 1935 to 1937. In this period it became apparent that certain cartels were using their powers to maintain prices artifically in a deflationary situation. To correct this undesirable state of affairs, a large number of cartels and syndicates were compelled, in December, 1935, to reduce their prices either by voluntary agreement or by the forcible dissolution of the syndicates responsible for price maintenance. Out of 154 cartels and syndicates which came under government scrutiny, some 79 were dissolved. This action was backed up by the further threat that if Polish industrial prices were not brought into line with international prices, the protective tariff would be suspended and foreign goods would be admitted at a low customs duty in order that the people could satisfy their requirements for industrial goods at reasonable prices. The resulting reductions in prices were not, however, all passed on to the final consumer. The Minister of Commerce and Industry then gave warning in his budget speech that unless the merchants and distributors reduced their profit margins the government would take the further step of controlling traders' profits.

Subsequently, the minister of commerce dissolved 118 cartels, mostly for maintaining economically unjustifiable prices. The effects of government policy were, moreover, not fully revealed by the official statistics, for some cartels, when threatened with forcible liquidation, preferred to dissolve themselves voluntarily. It can thus reasonably be argued that the tendency in Polish industry toward cartellization—a tendency inherited from the days of partition (the first cartels in the Polish heavy industries were formed in 1880)—was manipulated by the Polish government to obtain the maximum economic gain—the preservation and utilization of existing capital and the maintenance of employment—while the consumers' interests were protected, whenever it became apparent that the cartels were attempting to maintain economically unjustifiable prices, by the exercise in a drastic and exemplary fashion of the powers of cartel dissolution placed in the hands of the minister of commerce.

The culmination of the industrial development of Poland in this period was the foundation of the Central Industrial District started in the middle of 1936. As an example of the state planning of economic life within the limits of a fairly free capitalist framework, its lessons are of the first importance to all students of the problems of the relative roles of the state and free enterprise in economic development. In the first place, in order to get the perspective right, it should be made clear that the industrial development of the Warsaw-Cracow-Lwów triangle alone was not in itself the primary objective of the plan. That development was planned as an integral factor in the complete reorganization of the Polish economic system as an organic whole; a necessity if the basic social problem of the country—an imbalance between the agricultural and industrial sectors of the national economy—was to be solved on a permanent and satisfactory basis. The development of the Central Industrial District must therefore be seen as leading up to the Fifteen-Year Plan of Minister Kwiatkowski which was intended to develop through the following phases:

Year	Primary emphasis
(1) 1939–1942	Increase of war potential
(2) 1942–1945	Provision of adequate transportation facilities
(3) 1945–1948	Improvement of agriculture and intensification of production
(4) 1948–1951	Industrialization and urbanization
(5) 1951–1954	The balancing and completion of the new economic structure of the country

The Central Industrial District, situated around the confluence of the Vistula and the San, had an area of some 60,000 square kilometers and a population of something like 5,500,000. It was one of the most poverty-stricken areas in the country with an extremely dense peasant population living in conditions of great economic distress. Rural overpopulation for the area was estimated at some 400,000. Yet the region was potentially rich, for it had considerable natural resources and good agricultural land. It fell, economically, into three divisions: (1) Kielce, rich in minerals; (2) Lublin, suitable for agriculture; and (3) Sandomierz, suitable for processing industries. The Central Industrial District thus formed a naturally well balanced geographical and economic unit. Under the partitioning powers, it had been on the frontiers of two of the powers and thus had been neglected economically. Indeed, the position had been in reality somewhat worse, since for military reasons the area had been almost completely deprived of communications. The roads across the frontiers were often not connected; the railways ran parallel to the frontiers instead of across them; and the Vistula was cut politically into three parts and was neglected as a navigable waterway. The Czarist government, indeed, had looked with active hostility upon any attempt to develop the

97

navigability of the river. Before the partitions, the area had been a center of Polish commerce and industry. The partitions had turned it into an economically depressed area, and its misery was further increased after 1919 by the virtual cessation of Polish immigration into the U.S.A., Canada, and Brazil.

In the light of the industrial tradition of the area in the period from the sixteenth to the eighteenth centuries, of the plentiful natural resources to be found there, of the state of extreme misery resulting from the faulty demographic structure of the area, and of the deliberate neglect of its economic possibilities by the partitioning powers, it was natural that the attention of Polish economists should be turned to the problems of this region. A law of 1928 had granted tax exemptions and reductions to industrial enterprises founded in the region north of Sandomierz, and rough plans for the economic development of the area were sketched out at about the same time. Tax relief, however, proved an insufficient inducement to attract industry to the neighborhood. Then the onset of the general economic depression ruled out for some years the possibility of positive state intervention. It was not until 1936 that steps could be taken to implement the tentative plans which had been first considered some eight or nine years before.

Apart from the economic attractions of the proposal, there were by 1936 important military reasons for concentrating the heavy armament and allied industries in an area away from the frontiers. The old industrial centers, although they obviously presented the usual advantages of economies external to the firm but internal to the region, were dangerously close to the western frontiers which would almost certainly be speedily overrun by a German invading force. The Central Industrial District, however, if planned as a whole on the basis of new communications and of a "grid" for the supply of electricity and gas to the whole region could be made to yield many of these locational economies. Its development would not only meet the needs of national defense and relieve the miseries of a backward area but could also be made the first step in the necessary economic transformation of the whole country. Moreover, it would at the same time link the highly industrialized Silesian area with the industrially backward area of Volhynia.

The state did not intend, however, to monopolize the whole of industry in the area. The development of the region was to be the result of a partnership between the state and private enterprise. Apart from the erection of a large-scale state armaments industry, the government was to equip the area with satisfactory communications—road, rail, and water—and to provide a "grid" for the supply of electric power and gas. Industrialists were to be granted tax exemptions and special credits, grants, and privileges. There was in consequence an influx of private enterprise into the area, while at the same time certain plants were "mixed" enterprises, owned partly by the government and partly by private firms.

The successful development of the Central Industrial District showed that the Poles had both the imaginative and executive powers for successfully carrying out large-scale economic planning. The importance of these qualities was becoming very apparent by 1939, for by then it had become clear that the success of the economy of the Central Economic District implied the control of the whole national economy. This fact was brought to the front by the problem of the import of industrial raw materials and machinery. Such necessary imports threw a great strain on the balance of trade, especially as the process of industrialization contributed to the lack of export surpluses, and the problem of providing foreign raw materials and machinery became increasingly acute. Foreign exchange rates had been controlled in April, 1936, but this measure alone was not adequate. To meet the problems raised by increasing

99

industrialization, foreign trade had to be put on a quota and clearing basis, and consumption had to be controlled by means of forced saving. The ramifications of planning the Central Industrial District were clearly transforming the whole national economy to a planned economy when that development was ruthlessly cut short by foreign invaders in September, 1939.

CHAPTER 8

The Organization
of Commerce

THE ORGANIZATION of commerce in Poland was profoundly
affected by two historical factors: the position of the towns in
the social structure of the country and the position of the Jews
in the community. In the Middle Ages, Polish towns and their
burghers had prospered exceedingly by the growth of commerce arising from the crossing of Poland by important trade
routes. The zenith of their development was toward the end of
the fifteenth century. Developments in the sixteenth century split
them off from the rest of the social organism, and they came to
hold an isolated and exclusive position. Laws of 1505, 1538, and
1550 forbade the gentry, under penalty of losing their rights and
privileges, to engage in industry or commerce.

From this period onward, a barrier grew up between the
towns—the centers of commerce—and the rest of the Polish
nation. The commercial centers found themselves in a socially
artificial position, deriving from the fact that they became alien
bodies in, but not of, the social organism, yet retaining the
right to live off it. Thus, whereas in other countries the growth
of commerce brought increasing wealth and social progress
and made for increasing national unity (for example, the atti-

101

tude of the English nobility and gentry toward the commercial classes which was shown in a transference between and an inter-mingling of the different social groups), in Poland the towns and the commercial groups inhabiting them became a source of social disunity and emphasized the clash of rival social and economic groups and of alien minorities with the vast body of the people.

The bad social and economic effects resulting from this first factor were accentuated by the peculiar position of the Jews in Poland. Again, the problem is one which has its roots in the Middle Ages. It dates from the period when persecuted Jews, fleeing from the countries of western Europe, found refuge in Poland where they were hospitably received and were allowed to settle on liberal conditions of self-government. The Jews were welcomed not merely from humanitarian motives, however, but because it was realized that they were bringing business ex-perience, enterprise, and capital into the country. Their admis-sion into Poland on favorable terms had thus a sound economic justification. The resulting segregation of the Jews into the towns emphasized, however, the separation of the towns from the general body of the nation and, unfortunately, laid the seeds for future economic trouble by bringing into existence something very like a Jewish monopoly of trade. The position was made worse by the Czarist policy of persecuting the Jews, a policy which during the nineteenth century caused a migration of Jews into Russian Poland from Russia proper, and this second wave had to be superimposed upon the earlier Jewish immigration from western Europe. Thus, in addition to the crowded ghettos of central Poland, there came into existence a congestion of the Jewish population in the towns on the eastern border; for ex-ample, towns such as Pinsk found themselves with Jewish ma-jorities of 80 and 90 per cent. The economic result was that the new republic found that while the Jewish elements constituted less than 10 per cent of the total population, they controlled nearly half the commercial enterprises of the country. The nature of the problem may be seen from Tables 38 and 39.

TABLE 38. OCCUPATIONAL STRUCTURE OF THE POLISH POPULATION.

Category	Percentage of total population
Agriculture	63
Industry	20
Trade, communications, professions, education	17

TABLE 39. OCCUPATIONAL STRUCTURE OF POLISH JEWRY.*

Category	Percentage of total population
Agriculture	0.7
Industry	20.3
Commerce	58.0
Profession, education	21.0

* Polish Jewry made up 9.8 per cent of the total population.

Some industries were almost completely dominated by Jews, for example, 94.7 per cent of the textile industry and 95.6 per cent of the leather and fur industry. The typical economic position of the Polish Jew was that of the small entrepreneur, and the concentration of two-thirds of the Jewish population within the cities presented a difficult problem in a country which had over 60 per cent of its total population engaged in agriculture, since the position of Jews in commerce and handicrafts blocked the natural channels of economic expansion of the non-Jew. The Polish peasant, for example, who wished to migrate to the town from the overpopulated countryside found it virtually impossible, in the face of Jewish preponderance, to establish himself in handicraft industry or in shopkeeping, the two economic activities which presented the most natural openings for him. Buell observes:

While the Jews constitute less than 10 per cent of the population, they control nearly half the commercial enterprises of Poland; 47 per cent of the artisans, half the lawyers, and a large percentage of the doctors are Jews.

More than half the textile industry in Lodz is Jewish; and some estimate that half the real property in Warsaw and other cities is also Jewish . . .

Although the Jews dominate many branches of economic life, the gradual processes of economic and social development are tending to reduce this predominance. . . .[1]

This economic imbalance presented not merely economic problems, however, but led to serious social tensions. Moreover, it must be admitted that some restrictive policies of sucessive Polish ministries in this period led easily to the charge of anti-Semitism. The problem was essentially one of making the best of an unfortunate historical legacy; that it was extremely complicated and did not yield to simple measures quickly only intensified popular exasperation (for the most part unjustified) at an unpopular minority. It would be completely incorrect, however, to identify the policies of, say, the Pilsudski regime toward the Jews with the anti-Semitism of Hitler, Goebbels, and Streicher.

When we look at the percentage of the population actively engaged in employment, we find that the numbers employed in the distributive services and in trade exceeded those employed in factory industry and almost equaled the figure for the whole of industry. Detailed figures are given in Table 40.

That the small unit was the representative economic unit in Polish trade is seen when we look at the statistics for retail trade. In 1938, there were 374,153 retail shops in the country. Of this

[1] R. L. Buell, *Poland: Key to Europe* (London, 1939), p. 298.

TABLE 40. DISTRIBUTION OF EMPLOYED POPULATION IN TRADE AND INDUSTRY (1931).

Category	Percentage of employed population
Distributive services	9.7
Trade	5.3
Industry	16.7
Factory industry	12.0

total, 344,346 were one-man enterprises. Their distribution by type of trade is particularly enlightening.

TABLE 41. DISTRIBUTION OF RETAIL TRADE IN POLAND (1938).

Category	Percentage
Foodstuffs	57.3
Clothing	20.4
Building materials and fuel	4.5
Iron and metal goods	3.6
Chemical products	3.3
Furniture and household goods	2.6
Paper, books, periodicals	2.2
Not classified	6.1

So far as the actual structure of trade is concerned, certain commercial organizations must be mentioned. A law of 1921, which was modified by presidential decrees in 1924 and 1928, laid the legal foundations for the creation of produce exchanges. These bodies were organized as closed corporations under government supervision which was exercised through commissioners of the Ministry of Industry and Trade. Agricultural produce exchanges were organized in Warsaw, Cracow, Lwów, and Poznan, timber exchanges at Bydgoszcz and Warsaw, and a meat exchange in Warsaw. The textile exchange at Lodz had to be closed down. Katowice, however, received an agricultural exchange.

There had been many voluntary associations of merchants in Poland as far back as the fifteenth century, as in Cracow, Poznan, and Lwów. After 1905 in Russian Poland, voluntary associations of Polish merchants came into being again, and this development continued rapidly under the new republic. Local organizations and regional unions were added to the older associations. Finally, in 1925, the Congress of Polish Merchants created a supreme council as the joint representative body of all Polish merchant associations.

In addition to the voluntary associations, there were official chambers of commerce. They had been unknown in Russian Poland but had existed in the Prussian and Austrian areas. A presidential decree of 1927 extended their organization, which was at the same time made uniform, to the whole country. They included many activities in their program, such as the organization of commercial exhibitions and conferences, the publication of commercial periodicals, the development of foreign trade relations, the organization of commercial schools, and the development of the tourist traffic. They also kept a fostering eye on the development of the new produce exchanges and the stock exchanges. In 1938, there were chambers of commerce in Warsaw, Sosnowiec, Lodz, Lublin, Lwów, Cracow, Poznan, Wilno, Gdynia, and Katowice.

The tendency toward increasing state intervention in economic matters, to which attention has been called already in the chapters on banking and industry, was also found in the sphere of commerce. In 1937, the state began to intervene in marketing. Wholesale and retail prices were fixed for cereals, meat, milk, lard, and butcher's pork; and loans were granted on special terms against corn, hops, and flax fibers in order to promote orderly marketing. This measure was in the interest of the peasant producer who, otherwise, was in danger of the forced

106

sale of his product on unfavorable terms to speculators. Finally, the National Industrial and Cereals Company, an official organization, was set up with the sole right of exporting the wheat surplus and with a part to play in regulating the distribution of grain on the internal market.

The most outstanding feature of commercial organization in Poland, however, was the co-operative movement, with its two main divisions into agricultural co-operative societies and consumer co-operative societies, to which were joined such less important co-operatives as military and minor manufacturing co-operative societies.

As long ago as the beginning of the eighteenth century attempts had been made in Poland to run economic enterprises on co-operative principles. These early beginnings were, however, of no great economic significance. It was not until the period immediately after the defeat of the 1863 insurrection, when the Polish nation turned from romantic and idealistic dreams to a policy of "organic work" and of political compromise, that the real foundations of a Polish co-operative movement were laid.

In 1869, three consumer co-operatives were started in Russian Poland. A year later a consumer co-operative was started in Austrian Poland, and the following year saw one established in Prussian Poland. By 1900, Poland had about 100 societies with a membership of approximately 10,000. After the revolutionary upheaval in Russia in 1905, there was a considerable growth in the co-operative movement in Russian Poland, where it rapidly reached a membership of some 100,000 split among 1,700 societies. In 1911 came the first union of consumer co-operatives, the Warsaw Union (commonly known as *Spolem*), extending to all parts of Russian Poland. Two years later, there came into being a co-operative union for Austrian Poland with its headquarters in Lwów. During the last phases of the 1914 to 1918 war the various co-operative societies played an important part in the distribution of food, and on November 1, 1918 there opened in Lublin an all-Poland congress of representatives of the co-operative societies with the purpose of formulating the main principles which should guide the co-operative movement in the new republic. It is perhaps worth quoting the following few sentences from the declaration of principles which was adopted:

The congress recognizes that the basic economic principle of co-operation is the socialization of the means of production and exchange in the interests of labor. With this in mind, in all their fields of activity, the consumer societies should disavow the capitalistic system of economy, which has as its end not the consumption of commodities but profit arising from the possession of capital.

The position of co-operative societies in the new republic was regulated by the law of 1920 which, with only minor changes, governed the position over the whole period under consideration. The law formally defined a co-operative, laid down the principles on which co-operatives had to be established, and set out methods for their supervision. The basic principles applied were open membership, a democratic structure—one member, one vote—and restrictions on interest on shares. The law also provided for the union of the various societies in auditing unions and for the creation of a State Co-operative Council attached to the Ministry of Finance. The movement progressed so strongly that by the end of 1937 there were approximately 14,000 co-operative societies with a membership of over three million. These societies divided into the groups shown in Table 42.

Co-operation enables small agriculturists to get together and to solve successfully problems which otherwise would defeat them. This basic fact was well brought out in Poland in the development, first, of credit co-operatives to defeat the exploitation of the peasants by the moneylenders, next in the creation of co-operatives for the disposal of agricultural produce and the

108

TABLE 42. ORGANIZATION OF POLISH CO-OPERATIVE SOCIETIES (DECEMBER 31, 1938).*

Type	Number
Consumers	2,137
Agricultural consumers	3,207
Agricultural trading	453
Dairying	1,475
Credit	5,597
Housing	261
Others	611
Total	13,741

* *Source:* Extracted from *Concise Statistical Year-Book of Poland, 1939–41*, p. 49, table 16.

purchase of equipment, and finally in the co-operative organization of the processing of agricultural produce so that it could be disposed of in the final form suitable for the ultimate consumer. Simultaneously, with the co-operative organization of production went the co-operative organization of consumption, just as important in rural as in urban areas.

The agricultural co-operatives were organized in one auditing union with headquarters in Warsaw. This "Union of Agricultural Co-operatives of the Polish Republic" was divided into nine provincial unions with headquarters at Bialystok, Cracow, Lublin, Lwów, Luck, Poznan, Torun, Warsaw, and Wilno. At the end of December, 1937, the union had a membership of 1,645,000 split up among 5,497 societies. Details are given in Table 43.

The consumers' societies, after fulfilling a very useful social purpose in the distribution of food toward the end of the 1914–1918 war, had a very checkered career during the period of the first postwar inflation. The stabilization of the currency found them with their capital so seriously reduced that they had to start practically from the beginning again in building

TABLE 43. MEMBERSHIP OF THE AGRICULTURAL UNION OF
CO-OPERATIVES (DECEMBER, 1937).

Type of co-operative	Number of societies	Membership
Savings and credit	3,396	1,061,000
Trading and consumers societies	775	129,000
Dairy farming	1,166	430,000
Not classified	160	25,000
Total	5,497	1,645,000

up the confidence of their members. The working-class co-operatives had started to organize themselves independently of the older societies in a separate Union of Worker Consumer Co-operatives. In 1925, however, this body joined with the old-established Warsaw Union, and the resulting body took the name of the Union of Consumer Societies of the Polish Republic. In the next year, the union was joined by the Group of Consumer Co-operatives of State and Local Government Employees and by the Central Organization of Consumer Co-operative Associations of Christian Workers. Thus, from 1926 onward, there was only the one consolidated Union of Consumer Co-operatives of the Polish Republic (or *Spolem* for short). This body made exceedingly good progress, despite all the difficulties arising from the economic crisis of 1929 onward. By 1939, it had extended its activities into all parts of the country and into most spheres of co-operative production and distribution. It had thirty-two branches and twenty-six warehouses. It possessed three branches for the purchase of agricultural produce, a textiles branch, a coffee roasting and packing plant at Gdynia, fruit and vegetable canning and preserving works, fish curing and packing works, soap and pharmaceutical plants, pickle and condiment factories, yeast works, a sawmill, cabinet-making factories, and various bakeries and factories for making

110

household requisites. Its wholesale activities may be judged from Table 44.

TABLE 44. WHOLESALE ACTIVITIES OF *Spolem* (1938).

Commodity	Metric tons
Sugar	23,654
Salt	37,392
Coal and coke	72,910
Matches (in boxes)	14,975
Wheat flour	10,926
Rye flour	6,432
Barley	4,628
Rice	3,192
Herrings (barrels)	16,014
Tea	82
Coffee	129
Yeast	189
Cement	18,934
Chemical fertilizers	27,347
Petroleum	7,534

The union had at the end of 1938 a membership of 395,630 split up among 1,886 societies. Thirty-one per cent of the members were industrial workers, and 44 per cent were agricultural workers. The remainder fell into various social groups.

In addition to the main co-operative societies, there were certain minor co-operative enterprises which perhaps deserve mention for the sake of completeness. The Union of Employees Co-operative Societies and Associations brought together some 625 societies, of which 243 were savings and credit societies, 294 were building societies, 58 dwellings societies, and 30 manufacturing societies. The 243 savings and credit societies had over 97,000 members and a capital of some 12 million zloty. The military co-operative societies, federated in the Auditing Union of Military Co-operatives, had a membership of 26,000 spread over 204 consumers societies which carried on 370 shops, 7 bakeries, and 4 butcher shops. The principle of dividing the trading surplus of the military co-operatives is worth noting— 25 per cent went to reserves, 28 per cent to co-operative propaganda and education among soldiers, and the residual part to dividends on members' purchases and on additional wages to employees.

The national minorities had their own co-operative societies. The most outstanding were the Ukrainian societies, federated in their own Auditing Union with its headquarters at Lwów. This body had a membership in 1937 of 587,000 spread over 3,331 societies, of which 2,255 were consumers' societies, 668 were credit societies, 144 were dairy co-operatives, and 77 were handicraft societies. The Ukrainian societies were outstanding, despite the poverty of the members, for their tendency to build up reserve funds for the further development of the co-operative movement. The Jewish co-operatives developed in close connection with the *Bund* (the Jewish-Socialist Party) and between 1925 and 1930 a number of Jewish producers co-operatives sprang up. The most flourishing of the Jewish societies, however, were the building societies which built workers' houses (chiefly blocks of apartments). The co-operative societies of the German minority were mainly of the agricultural trading and credit type, federated in two organizations—the Union of German Co-operatives in Poland and the Union of Rural Co-operatives in Pomorze.

To sum up the economic significance of the various types and groupings of co-operative societies in Poland, we may say that the credit co-operative societies were the best developed. In 1939, there were 3,700 small village co-operative societies, which were banks of the Rieffeisen type and which were known as "Stefczyk" banks after Stefczyk, the great pioneer of co-operation in Poland, and there were in addition about 1,600 larger people's banks of the Schultze-Delitzsch type in the smaller towns and villages. By providing an acceptable means for the accumulation of local savings—they accepted and paid interest on even very small deposits—these societies brought into action local funds which would not otherwise have been used productively in the locality, a very important contribution to the economic prosperity of the country when we remember the ever-present dearth of capital in Poland. They also distributed the loans from the state banks and the public funds placed at the disposal of agriculturists. The agricultural and trading societies were less developed than the credit co-operatives. They performed two main economic functions: first, the supply of agrarian materials and equipment, for example, fertilizers, fuel, machinery, and, second, the marketing of agricultural products, especially cereals, cattle, and pigs. Last came the manufacturing co-operative societies which had an importance transcending mere trading transactions, for, by engaging in processing, they created fresh market openings for the utilization of agricultural raw materials. The typical example of this type of society was the dairy co-operative.

We may say as a general conclusion that co-operative organization enabled the Polish peasant to counteract the economic disadvantage of the breakup of the large estates, for so long as the peasant was unorganized his economic independence and standard of living were threatened by the pressure of organized industry operating to produce a still greater disparity between industrial and agricultural prices. Co-operation enabled the individual small farmer to cope with problems which might easily otherwise have overwhelmed and destroyed him.

CHAPTER 9

The Search for Markets

IF THE Polish people were to enjoy a standard of living above a bare subsistence level, Poland could not be self-sufficient: a policy of autarchy for Poland would have been the road to economic extinction. That is a blunt and basic fact which must be faced by all who have to deal with the economic development of modern Poland. Because of the narrowing of the world market to one of would-be self-sufficient national groups, Poland before the war of 1939 to 1945 had nearly a quarter of its population living close to starvation. A freely functioning world economy in which Poland could export enough of its agricultural and industrial products to pay for the imports of raw materials and machinery necessary for the industrialization of the country, in which foreign capital could flow easily into the country, and in which some of its surplus population could migrate freely to other countries was a necessary condition for the prosperity of Poland. The struggle for markets was, therefore, of critical importance.

Geographically, Poland is well placed to be a center for international trade. It will be recalled from Chapter 1 that for many centuries Poland had been a thriving center of international commerce and that the decline came as the deliberately planned result of, first, Prussian policy in the eighteenth century, and, later, the policies of the partitioning powers.

One of the most urgent problems facing the new republic in 1919 was the restoration of foreign trade, since, apart from the immediate needs for rehabilitation and reconstruction, the industrial development of the newly restored state was largely dependent on foreign raw materials, foreign machinery, and foreign capital. That imports must be paid for by exports is an economic truism: Poland therefore had to export or perish. A very important complicating factor, which made the problem even more difficult of solution than would be imagined from the economic aspects alone, was that Poland's nearest neighbors, with whom she might normally have been expected to have had close trading relationships, were politically suspect to the new state. Having just escaped from 125 years of subjection and oppression by them, Poland could not with equanimity contemplate their continued dominance of her international trading relations.

For the purposes of studying the trends in foreign trade, we may most conveniently divide the period under consideration into three—1918 to 1925, 1925 to 1936, and 1936 to 1939. In the first period, foreign trade was practically under complete government control. It was a period characterized by short-term quota agreements for the direct exchange of commodities on a barter basis. One of the first acts of the new republic was to impose in November, 1919, a general customs tariff based on the Russian tariff of 1903. This act was an interim measure to cover the period in which a foreign trade policy could be conceived and created. Germany and Russia were politically suspect; hence, Poland hastened to establish commercial relations with her political allies in order to ensure her economic development independent of her powerful neighbors. Commercial treaties, based on the most-favored-nation principle, were concluded with France, Rumania, Italy, Belgium, Yugoslavia, Switzerland, the United Kingdom, Turkey, and Austria. So far as Germany was concerned, the economic clauses of the Treaty

115

of Versailles made it obligatory for her to grant up to January 10, 1925, unilateral most-favored nation treatment to the Allied and associated powers, which included Poland. Moreover, natural or manufactured products from Polish territories which had been under German occupation before the war were to be exempted from all German customs duties for a period of three years. The main factor governing foreign trade in this early period, however, was the progressive inflation of the Polish currency, which gave an artificial stimulus to the export trades. This factor can be overemphasized, however, for it must be remembered that in the immediate postwar period inflation of an even more galloping kind than that in Poland developed in many of its neighbors, for example, in Germany, Austria, Hungary, and Czechoslovakia, while in Russia conditions were more unsettled than anywhere else. In these areas, which were the natural areas for the development of Polish trade, the Polish exporter was faced with the danger of obtaining payment in a depreciated currency of even less value than his own. The stimulus which would otherwise have been provided by inflation was thus counteracted for trade with these countries by the even more inflated state of their own currencies. In spite of transit difficulties with Germany and Czechoslovakia, certain industries—especially the textile industries of Lodz—gained ground in foreign markets. This artificial boom in the export trades was sharply brought to an end by the stabilization of the currency at a relatively high exchange rate by Grabski.

Even before Grabski's financial reforms, however, a changed trend was apparent in the course of Poland's foreign trade. In 1922, a commercial treaty had been signed with France according to which there were reductions in the "general" tariff of between 25 per cent and 50 per cent on a number of French commodities. This break in the tariff was followed in 1924 by the negotiation of tariff conventions with France and with Czechoslovakia. Friendly economic relations were established with

Russia by which, in exchange for orders placed with Polish industries, the U.S.S.R. was granted import quotas and preferential duties on certain specified imports. Export activity was directed especially toward the Baltic and Scandinavian countries, and in this connection Poland had a lucky break in the British coal dispute of 1926. The temporary cessation of British coal exports gave the Polish coal industry an opportunity of seizing export markets hitherto dominated by Great Britain—an opportunity which was successfully exploited. During this second period, Poland's foreign-trade relations showed some tendency toward becoming dangerously overdependent on the trade agreements with France and Czechoslovakia, but the essential economic strength of the new republic was clearly demonstrated in the tariff war with Germany, the most important event in Poland's international trading relations at this time.

Let us make no mistake about the seriousness of this struggle—in the tariff war with Germany, Poland was fighting for her economic independence. Germany was exercising the full strength of her economic power for the achievement of noneconomic ends. The use of economic penetration to undermine a country's political independence is not an invention of Hitler's. It was advocated and practiced by such "good" Germans as Gustav Stresemann; for example, in his speech of September 7, 1925, he declared, "The third great task . . . is the readjustment of our Eastern frontiers, the recovery of Danzig, the Polish corridor and a correction of the frontier in Upper Silesia." The tariff war had actually broken out some months previously in June, 1925, and German intentions had been clearly stated in the *Frankfurter Zeitung* of June 14, 1925:

Either Poland will embark upon an absolute economic war with us (which will injure us also, but which we shall come through) and a great part of her coal and timber industry will be ruined or she will sign a treaty such as we desire. In either case, Poland will come out of this war mortally wounded. She will lose her strength and finally

117

also her independence—and then in a few years, together with Russia, we shall administer the *coup de grâce*.

It was in such prophetic words that a great "liberal" newspaper set out the policy which was later to be put into effect so successfully by Hitler and Stalin.

The Polish coal, zinc, and iron industries were adversely affected. On the other hand, the Polish market was an important one for German manufactured goods. The various measures and countermeasures thus caused economic hardships to both sides, but, paradoxical as it may seem, Polish industry and commerce probably benefited from the blows, for they revealed in an unmistakable manner the danger of economic dependence on Germany. It is from this period that date the rapid growth of Poland's maritime trade and the development of her own port of Gdynia and her own merchant fleet. Instead of accomplishing the ruin of Poland's trade, the tariff war actually extended the scope of Poland's international trade by forcing Polish merchants to seek other markets overseas. In this connection, we are reminded of the economically beneficial outcome of German attempts to buy up Polish lands and so drive out the Poles at the end of the nineteenth century. On each occasion a German policy aimed at ruining the Poles had the ultimate and unexpected result of benefiting them economically.

After several abortive attempts at ending the tariff war, notably the commercial treaty of March 17, 1930, which was ratified by the Poles but thrown out by the Reichstag, the struggle was brought to an end by the *Zollfriedensprotokoll* of March 7, 1934, which ended the many restrictions and prohibitions put into force by both countries.

The new policy, which characterized the third phase of foreign-trade policy during this period from 1919 to 1939, was marked by a broadening of Poland's international trading relations. Gdynia and the Polish mercantile marine had developed. The development of the Central Industrial District was under way. There was no longer any doubt of the economic strength and stability of the new republic, both of which had been reasonably open to doubt in 1925. The tariff war had also brought readjustments in Germany which, by increasing her own production of foodstuffs, had reduced the necessity of further imports of supplies previously obtained from Poland. The hitherto economic interdependence of the two countries had thus been greatly lessened by the tariff war, and new international economic relations had come into being, notably with Great Britain. A trade agreement on a limited most-favored-nation basis, valid for one year, but with a proviso for revision and automatic extension, was signed with Germany on November 4, 1934. Its importance was overshadowed, however, by the Anglo-Polish Trade Agreement of 1935 and by a commercial convention signed with Canada. These two agreements helped Poland to achieve a greater measure of independence in her trade policy and lessened the preponderance of the agreements with France and Czechoslovakia, which had, however, been already somewhat weakened by a commercial treaty with Belgium and by tariff protocols with Sweden, Holland, and Switzerland.

Although the broadening of Poland's foreign trade had removed one weakness, the years after 1936 revealed another source of danger. It was in 1936 that a policy of large-scale, planned industrialization had been decided upon. Poland had no manganese, nickel, copper, tin, aluminum, rubber, or cotton. Polish iron ore was of low quality, and native-produced wool was negligible. If the new policy were to be carried through, there would have to be large imports of essential raw materials and machinery. Industrial raw materials in fact accounted for half of Polish imports at this time, and when added to the machinery and capital which had to be imported they threw a great burden on Poland's balance of trade. The problem of stepping up exports to pay for imports became one of first urgency and was rendered even more difficult by two facts: the value of agricultural exports per unit quantity was far lower than in the period before the great slump in agricultural prices which had accompanied the world economic crisis, and, second, the maintenance of the zloty at an overvalued exchange rate handicapped the export trades very severely.

The result of this set of circumstances was the complete abandonment in 1936 of a traditional laissez-faire policy in Poland's international economic relations. Between April and July, 1936, the Polish government issued decrees which introduced exchange control, placed all imports and exports under severe control, and suspended payments on its foreign debt. It then began the negotiation of clearing agreements in order to balance as closely as possible imports and exports country by country. By 1938, there were ten clearing agreements covering about 28 per cent of Poland's foreign trade. The proof of the pudding is in the eating. What were the results of the changes in foreign trade policy which have just been described? That question is best answered by looking at the foreign trade figures set out in Table 45.

TABLE 45. POLAND'S FOREIGN TRADE (IN MILLIONS OF ZLOTY) (1922–1938).*

Year	Imports	Exports	Total	Balance
1922	1,453.0	1,126.0	2,579.0	—327.0
1923	1,939.0	2,005.0	3,994.0	66.0
1924	2,544.9	2,176.8	4,721.7	—368.1
1925	2,756.2	2,187.4	4,943.6	—568.8
1926	1,540.7	2,245.8	3,786.5	705.1
1927	2,892.0	2,514.7	5,406.7	—377.3
1928	3,362.2	2,508.0	5,870.2	—854.2
1929	3,112.6	2,813.2	5,925.8	—299.4
1930	2,245.9	2,433.2	4,679.1	187.3
1931	1,468.2	1,878.6	3,346.8	410.4
1932	862.0	1,083.8	1,945.8	221.8
1933	827.0	960.0	1,787.0	133.0

Year	Imports	Exports	Total	Balance
1934	799.0	975.0	1,774.0	176.0
1935	861.0	925.0	1,786.0	64.0
1936	1,003.0	1,026.0	2,029.0	23.0
1937	1,254.0	1,196.0	2,460.0	−58.0
1938	1,300.0	1,185.0	2,485.0	−115.0

* This table has been compiled by using figures from two sources. For the years 1922 to 1932, the figures are those given by Casimir Smogorzewski in *Poland's Access to the Sea* (London: Allen & Unwin, 1934). For the years 1933 to 1938, the figures are those given by Leopold Wellisz in *Foreign Capital in Poland* (London: Allen & Unwin, 1938).

Table 45 is very illuminating in that it clearly shows the influences of changes in the exchange value of the zloty and of the economic crisis of the early 1930's as well as the increasing strain on the Polish balance of international payments in the years after 1934/1935, caused by the policy of increasing the pace of industrialization.

The distribution of Poland's foreign trade among countries is also of some interest and is set out in Table 46.[1]

TABLE 46. POLAND'S FOREIGN TRADE BY COUNTRIES OF ORIGIN AND DESTINATION (1938).*

Country	Percentage of total imports	Percentage of total exports
Germany	23.0	24.1
Great Britain	11.4	18.2
U.S.A.	12.2	5.3
Sweden	3.5	6.0
Belgium	4.1	4.8
Italy	2.6	5.5
France	3.6	3.8
Netherlands	2.8	4.6

[1] The pattern of distribution by countries shown in Table 46 should be compared with that of the years after 1945 shown in Table 70, pp. 196–197.

TABLE 46 (*continued*). POLAND'S FOREIGN TRADE BY COUNTRIES OF ORIGIN AND DESTINATION (1938).*

Country	Percentage of total imports	Percentage of total exports
Czechoslovakia	3.1	3.6
Argentina	2.8	1.9
Others	30.9	22.2

*Source: Constructed from data in *Concise Statistical Year-Book of Poland, 1939–41,* p. 74, table 5.

Table 46 tells a very different story from the corresponding statistics for the early years of the Polish Republic when Germany, and later France and Czechoslovakia, were at different times in a dangerously dominant position. By 1938, Polish foreign trade policy had been successful in broadening its international trading relations.

To complete this chapter, reference must be made to the position of the ports of Danzig and Gdynia. In view of the dominating part played by Danzig in the history of Polish foreign trade from the thirteenth to the eighteenth centuries, it might have been expected that it would have played the same part after 1919. Political differences prevented this happening. For example, during the tariff war with Germany, Danzig played the German game. Moreover, the growth of commerce and industry in the new republic were such that Danzig alone was an inadequate outlet to the sea. The result was that the Polish government decided to build a port of its own. In the ten years from 1924 to 1934, a tiny fishing village was transformed into one of the largest and best-equipped harbors in Europe. In 1922, only 7.3 per cent of Poland's foreign trade went by sea. By 1938, the percentage had grown to 77.8 per cent, and Gdynia handled 46.2 per cent of the whole bulk of Poland's foreign trade. Regular shipping lines went to the ports of the Baltic, the North Sea, England, France, the Mediterranean, the Near East and

Palestine, North and South America, South and West Africa, and Asia. Gdynia served not only Poland but also Czechoslovakia, Rumania, Hungary, and Austria. Table 47 sets out the comparative figures for the two ports.

TABLE 47. FOREIGN TRADE (IN THOUSAND TONS) THROUGH GDYNIA
AND DANZIG (SELECTED YEARS, 1930–1938).*

Year	Imports		Exports		Total	
	Gdynia	Danzig	Gdynia	Danzig	Gdynia	Danzig
1930	343	732	2,932	7,331	3,275	8,063
1931	507	448	4,573	7,653	5,080	8,101
1932	347	345	4,547	5,122	4,894	5,467
1935	866	396	6,523	4,266	7,119	4,622
1936	1,161	526	6,260	4,423	7,421	4,949
1937	1,475	800	7,151	5,123	8,626	5,923
1938	1,299	832	7,414	5,150	8,713	5,982

* Source: Compiled from data in Concise Statistical Year-Book of Poland, 1939–41, p. 73, table 4.

That the two ports *both* reached a high level of development shows that, quite apart from political considerations, the decision to create Gdynia was a wise one, for Danzig alone would have been incapable of dealing with the great increase in commerce. The *two* ports were proved necessary. The creation of Gdynia was thus not merely one of the outstanding technical achievements of the years between the wars; it was a striking example of the foresightedness in economic matters of the Polish government.

CHAPTER 10

The Condition of the People

IN VARIOUS places in earlier chapters, passing mention has been made of certain aspects of the standard of living of the Polish people during this period. It is now time to consider this question in more detail, lest a misleading impression should be given by the presentation of solely the worst aspects, as in the description of peasant conditions on pages 71 and 72. A one-sided collection of horrors, as in Engels' famous *Condition of the Working Class in 1844,* is not history (though some otherwise well-informed writers of the Left seem to think it incumbent to continue the Engels tradition when they write of anything Polish).

In this connection, it is important always to remember the natural poverty of the country. The per capita national income of prewar Poland was far lower than that of such countries as Great Britain and France, to say nothing of the United States, and was higher only than such notoriously low-standard countries as Bulgaria. It has been observed, "Even before the crisis a poor Polish peasant lived below any accepted standard of human existence." [1]

Sufficiently exact statistical data, such as make possible the

[1] George Kagan, "Agrarian Régime of Pre-War Poland," *Journal of Central European Affairs,* Oct., 1943, p. 241.

124

precise calculation of reliable national income figures for industrial countries such as Great Britain, are lacking for Poland. The direct summation of personal incomes obtainable from income tax returns, wage statistics, and similar sources is not possible because of the predominance of farmers, independent workers, and small masters, whose incomes were not subject to income tax. Net income produced cannot be evaluated, on the other hand, because no census of production, which would provide a reliable estimate of the net value of output, was ever taken in Poland. Even if it had been, the predominance of independent craftsmen, small masters, and farmers would have presented an almost insoluble problem to the statistician. The statistics given in this chapter should therefore be used with caution, since they provide only a fragmentary account of the over-all situation. Nevertheless, they are, it is hoped, better than nothing and provide a useful check on merely subjective impressions of the standard of living which are the only other sources of information of the subject.

TABLE 48. INCOME CONSUMED, ASSESSED AT URBAN
RETAIL PRICES (1929).

Category	Zloty
Urban consumption	12,500,000
Rural consumption	11,000,000
Investment	2,100,000
Total	25,600,000

When it is remembered that, although farmers and their families made up 64 per cent of the population in 1929, they consumed only 47 per cent of the real income available, the relative poverty of the rural population can be visualized. The position became worse in the years after 1929 as the throes of the worst agricultural crisis in eighty years gripped the country.

In Table 49, figures on the *consumption* of the different economic and social groups are given—not their income which, for reasons given above, is not ascertainable. Savings have not been distributed among classes but have been kept as totals.

TABLE 49. DISTRIBUTION OF POLISH NATIONAL INCOME (1929).

Class	Zloty
Salary earners	2,500,000,000
Wage earners (excluding farm workers)	4,300,000,000
Farm workers	1,600,000,000
Independent workers Small employers	3,500,000,000
Small farmers	8,700,000,000
Large landowners	700,000,000
Entrepreneurs Professional workers	2,200,000,000
Government services (education)	400,000,000
Income saved	2,100,000,000
Private savings	700,000,000
Due to foreigners	400,000,000
Public savings	1,400,000,000

In Chapter 7, some account has been given of the living conditions of the small farmers and peasants. It is, unfortunately, almost impossible to generalize about the conditions of the peasantry. All authorities are in agreement that they were miserable by any western European or American standards. Perhaps the best summary is that given by Wilbert E. Moore:

Poland has been one of the outstanding examples in Eastern Europe of an agrarian economy unable to provide employment for many persons whose livelihood depends on agriculture. . . .

The types of farm labor, methods of payment, and considerations of labor relations and relative status all show remarkable heterogeneity in Poland. This is due not only to the divergent institutional

126

developments in the several sections of the country as they were molded along German, Austrian, or Russian lines, but also to the unequal economic organization and opportunities for employment. Despite this diversity, one type of labor arrangement was surprisingly common: that of the deputant worker. In both the formerly Russian and the formerly German sections the large estate depended primarily upon these fairly permanent workers for the bulk of their year-round labor supply. They usually received a small cash wage, but the larger amount of their income was derived from the dwelling furnished by the employer, a plot of land (usually for potatoes in the east), pasture for one or two cows, and allotments of cereals or possibly other foodstuffs. This general pattern was subject to many modifications, depending upon particular regions, size of estates, and so on. . . .

Since the independent proprietors of very small holdings had to seek wage labor to supplement the income from their cultivation, their position was very close to that of the deputantists. This similarity was especially marked when the small holders entered into contracts for annual employment, less sufficient time for cultivation of their own plots. Their independence owing to property rights in a small plot of ground was scarcely greater than that of the deputantist, and their security might be smaller. . . .[2]

Two-thirds of the agricultural population was underfed, and the same was true of the urban workers. In the case of peasants working dwarf holdings, especially in southern Poland, nutrition was extremely inadequate on every count. It is perhaps worth while to set out a comparison between average consumption per person of certain foodstuffs and "desirable" consumption.

To turn now to the position of the industrial worker, we find that his standard of living, though low, was still a good deal higher than that of the peasant and improved considerably over the period from 1928 to 1936.

[2] Wilbert E. Moore, *Economic Demography of Eastern and Southern Europe* (Geneva: League of Nations, 1945), pp. 224–225.

TABLE 50. AVERAGE CONSUMPTION PER PERSON OF CERTAIN FOODSTUFFS AND DESIRABLE CONSUMPTION (PREWAR).

Foodstuff	Actual consumption	Desirable consumption
	(In pounds or quarts annually)	
Wheat and rye	392	550
Maize	—	—
Potatoes	920 *	440
Sugar	27	60
Meat	50	88
Milk and milk products	550	660
Eggs	90	200
Animal fats ⎫ Vegetable oils ⎬	7	33
Vegetables ⎫ Fruit ⎬	145	265

* This figure includes potatoes fed to livestock.

TABLE 51. WAGES AND COST OF LIVING OF INDUSTRIAL WORKERS (1928–1936).

Year	Wages	Cost of living	Real wages
1928	100.0	100.0	100.0
1929	108.4	101.4	106.8
1930	108.1	94.2	114.5
1931	100.9	85.9	117.6
1932	92.8	78.2	118.7
1933	85.5	71.2	123.4
1934	82.0	66.5	123.4
1935	80.5	63.9	126.1
1936	80.3	60.9	132.0

Compared with weekly wages in, for example, Great Britain, the wages of the Polish workers were low—some 50 per cent of the workers in large- and medium-scale industry received wages of between ten and thirty zloty a week. On the other hand, the cost of living was also very low, and the trend toward continuous improvement in favor of the wage earner is clearly shown in Table 51, above. The weakness of this table, however, is that it does not take into account the number of partly or totally unemployed. It applies only to those employed and so is overfavorable for urban workers as a whole.

The number of hours worked per week was reasonable by western European standards. An 8-hour working day and a 48-hour week in industry and commerce was legally binding, as was an annual holiday with pay for both manual and nonmanual workers. In point of fact, over the ten years from 1928 to 1938, in only one of the major industries did the average number of hours worked per week reach 48. The statistics on this point are worth setting out in full as they show clearly how a shorter working week was used in the period of economic depression as an alternative to increasing the number of unemployed.

TABLE 52. AVERAGE NUMBER OF HOURS PER WEEK WORKED PER
WORKER IN PRINCIPAL INDUSTRIES (1928–1938).*

Year	General average	Stone, glass, ceramics	Metal, manu- facture	Chemical industry	Tex- tiles	Food	Tim- ber
1928	45.4	46.8	45.5	48.8	43.5	47.0	45.3
1929	44.8	46.6	45.1	48.5	41.0	47.0	45.2
1930	43.9	45.8	44.1	48.3	39.7	46.4	44.4
1931	43.3	44.9	43.4	47.0	40.7	44.5	43.3
1932	41.4	42.9	43.0	44.1	38.7	40.8	41.5
1933	41.5	43.1	43.1	44.0	39.7	38.5	41.7
1934	42.2	44.0	44.1	44.9	39.7	39.6	42.8
1935	42.6	44.0	44.3	45.1	40.1	40.1	43.2
1936	42.7	43.9	44.6	45.1	39.9	40.3	43.5
1937	43.3	44.2	45.0	46.1	40.6	42.0	43.5
1938	43.7	44.2	45.0	46.2	41.4	42.8	43.6

* *Source:* Based on *Concise Statistical Year-Book of Poland, 1939–41,* p. 114, table 6.

The industrial worker, like the peasant, was badly hit by the economic depression, though the fall in agricultural prices worked to his advantage as a consumer, as can readily be seen from Table 51. Unemployment was relatively severe in some industries, and although the depths of the economic depression in other respects were reached in 1934, unemployment continued to rise until 1937. The main cause of this state of affairs was the maintenance of the zloty at too high an exchange rate with a consequent heavy handicapping of the export industries. Persistence in this policy for so long was perhaps the major mistake in Polish economic policy over the whole period from 1919 to 1939. Some unemployment was "concealed unemployment" resulting from spreading work over the available working force and reducing the working week of those employed, as shown in Table 52, above. Actual unemployment figures (ignoring the "concealed unemployment") are set out in Table 53.

TABLE 53. UNEMPLOYMENT IN POLAND (1929–1938).*

Year	Number of unemployed
1929	185,000
1931	315,000
1932	220,000
1933	343,000
1934	414,000
1935	403,000
1936	466,000
1937	470,000
1938	456,000

* Source: Concise Statistical Year-Book of Poland, 1939–41, p. 115, table 11.

The relief of unemployment was one of the objectives that the Polish government had in mind when it embarked on the creation of the Central Industrial District.[3] In the years after

[3] See pp. 96–100 for further details on the Central Industrial District.

1936, public works provided considerable mitigation of the distress caused by unemployment, but, of course, they could not provide a remedy for a situation caused essentially by the overvaluation of the zloty. In 1938, for example, public works provided employment for about 250,000 workers. Thus, the figures in Table 53 would have been considerably higher in the absence of this government-provided employment. Insofar as the public works were to provide for the development of the Central Industrial District, they were more than mere relief works. They were truly creative in that they were providing employment and at the same time contributing to the revival of private enterprise, thus giving a cumulative booster shot to the economy.

Statistics relating to wages, hours of work, employment and unemployment never tell the whole story, however, so far as the condition of the people is concerned. They need to be supplemented by some account of the collective provision by the state for the welfare and social security of the workers. The Polish record was, considering the poverty of the country and its retarded economic development, extremely good in this respect, despite the fact that the ordinary government budget was maintained at a lower level than that of almost any other central European country and despite the high demands on state expenditure for purposes of national defense after the rise of Hitler.

The roots of an enlightened program of social welfare were laid by Daszynski, the Socialist leader of the first temporary government of Poland in November, 1918. Polish delegates were active on the Commission on International Labour Legislation in 1919 which worked out the principles and organization of the International Labour Organisation, and for the next twenty years a Polish representative sat on the governing body of the I.L.O. During the same period, Polish governments ratified twenty conventions of the I.L.O., accepted a number of recom-

131

mendations, and in some ways went even further in defending working-class interests.

Six of the conventions ratified by the Polish government related to the employment of children and young persons. The employment of children and young persons was regulated principally by the law of July 2, 1924, amended by the law of November 4, 1931, and by the order of the minister of social welfare of October 5, 1935, setting out the various occupations in which young persons could not be employed. Overtime work for young persons was not allowed, and the attendance of young workers at trade finishing schools was compulsory. This attendance (six hours a week) was counted as working time and paid for as such by the employer.

The I.L.O. convention concerning a weekly day of rest was ratified in 1924, but in point of fact the principle had been legally accepted by the Polish government some five years previously, in the law of December 18, 1919.

Three I.L.O. conventions relating to unemployment were ratified in 1924, although legislation on some of the points covered went back to 1919. There was a system of employment exchanges, and there were two schemes of unemployment insurance—one for manual workers and one for intellectual workers (a term which was interpreted very widely). The manual workers' scheme covered all over sixteen years of age who were employed in undertakings employing five or more people, but excluding agricultural workers and domestic servants. The contributions were 2 per cent of the salary or wages received, and three-quarters of the contribution was paid by the employer. Benefit, amounting to 30 per cent of the average weekly wage over the previous thirteen weeks, was paid for a period not exceeding thirteen weeks to every unemployed person who had been insured for not less than twenty-six weeks during the preceding year. Under the intellectual workers' scheme, the contribution was the same percentage of salary or wages as for the manual worker, but the employer's contribution was between 40 and 60 per cent of the contribution according to salary. Benefits of between 23 and 35 per cent of the average salary of the previous year's employment were paid for a period of from five to nine months, provided that the contributor had been insured for at least twelve months during the preceding two years. These schemes could not, of course, cope with the relief problem presented by persistent unemployment such as arose under the impact of the world economic crisis and prolonged depression, but what insurance scheme could have done?

The Polish government in 1924 ratified the I.L.O. convention concerning the right of association and combination of agricultural workers, but actually the right of association and combination had been granted to all citizens by the constitution of 1921. Under Polish legislation, agricultural and industrial workers both enjoyed the right to combine in trade unions, and registered trade unions had the exclusive power of concluding collective agreements with employers and employers' organizations.

Four I.L.O. conventions relating to workmen's compensation were ratified by the Polish government. The general position was that under the state general compulsory accident scheme a pension was provided for manual and nonmanual workers who were incapacitated by an industrial accident. In the event of total incapacitation, the pension was two-thirds of the average wage or salary over the preceding three years. If death resulted from an industrial accident, the dependent was entitled to a widow's or orphan's pension. Contributions under the scheme were paid by the employer alone and varied according to the accident risk involved in the particular industry. This scheme included domestic servants within its cover.

Other I.L.O. conventions ratified by Polish governments related to industrial hygiene and safety, the articles of agreement of seamen, the marking of weight on heavy packages, and the establishment of an international scheme for the maintenance

133

of rights under invalidity, old-age, widow's, and orphan's insurance.

The social welfare policy of Polish governments over this period was very enlightened in respect to the employment of women. There was a complete ban for women on underground work, the carrying of heavy weights, and working as dockers at Gdynia. Certain occupations in which they would come into contact with poisonous chemicals, such as white lead, were also forbidden to women. Women labor inspectors were employed to safeguard the interests of women and juvenile workers. The Working Women's Protection Act of 1924 made provisions for safeguarding the position of expectant mothers, placed upon employers the obligation to provide a factory crèche if they employed over one hundred women, and put a ban on night work for women and on their working under dangerous or insanitary conditions.

To ensure the enforcement of the various laws and decrees governing conditions of employment, factory inspection was established in January, 1919, and codified by a decree of 1927. Apart from the enforcement of the various enactments relating to social welfare, the factory inspectors had powers to issue regulations regarding the fencing of machinery, to forbid the use of certain dangerous raw materials, and to mediate in industrial disputes. The medical supervision of working conditions in factories and workshops was the responsibility of doctors attached to the Factory Inspection Department.

A law of May, 1922, provided for holidays with pay on an extensive scale for both manual and nonmanual workers—for adult manual workers the provision was for an eight-day holiday with pay annually after one year's work and for fifteen days after three years. Young workers were given fourteen days with pay after a year's work, and intellectual workers were entitled to one month's holiday with pay annually.

134

Registered trade unions and employers' organizations were given the exclusive right of making collective agreements which could not be replaced or superseded by an individual contract of employment. The terms of the collective agreement, which was registered with the appropriate factory inspector, applied not only to union men but also to nonunion men in the undertaking. Individual disputes between workers and employers in industry, commerce, and transport were dealt with by labor courts made up of a judge and two lay members selected by the minister of justice from a panel drawn up by the trade unions and employers' organizations. In agriculture, however, such disputes were dealt with in the first instance by the appropriate factory inspector, and then if he failed to secure agreement reference was made to a special arbitration board which included representatives of the trade unions and employers' organizations.

A system of compulsory sickness and maternity insurance was brought into being by the law of May, 1920. All manual and nonmanual workers, outdoor workers, and domestic servants whose wages did not exceed 125 zloty a month (say £6 or $24 a week) were included in it. Civil servants and local government employees were excluded, however, as were people engaged in casual employment. Contributions were 4.6 per cent of the wage, in the case of manual workers, and 5 per cent of the salary for nonmanual workers. Half the contribution was paid by the insured person and half by his employer. Wives and dependents were also included in the scheme. Agricultural workers, except in Upper Silesia, were not included but were covered by a separate scheme providing medical assistance and, if necessary, hospital treatment at their employer's expense. There were also schemes covering manual and nonmanual workers for invalidity and old age and providing benefits for their survivors in case of death. In 1934, all social insurance institutions were

135

placed under one uniform legal and administrative organization, and the pension-insurance schemes were extended to cover the whole country.

Thus a firm beginning of comprehensive measures of social welfare was made under the new republic in the years after 1920, even if the poverty of the country meant that the schemes could not be implemented as fast or as fully as might have been desired. Dr. Zweig's generalization seems not inaccurate on the record: "In the Twenty Years Poland built up a most progressive and comprehensive body of social legislation, hardly surpassed by any other country in the same stage of economic development. . . ." [4]

The social welfare program, however, can be legitimately criticized on the grounds of being overambitious and too bureaucratic. Again, to quote from Dr. Zweig:

It had also some drawbacks. It resulted in the setting up of a large body of bureaucrats and in heavy burdens being imposed on industry on the one side and on consumers' income on the other. Both workers and employers complained bitterly, the employers because of the sometimes extravagant claims for protection, of their high rates of contribution, and the great amount of control and statistics . . . ; the workers because they thought the social services rendered did not give full remunerative value for their contributions. There was a fair amount of red tape in the social services, which ate up a certain amount of the contributions, but during the last years a decided improvement in this regard took place.

The large capital funds collected in the Insurance institutions . . . were during the last years of the period under review borrowed by the State, which ended by imposing a strict control over the institutions concerned. . . .

The large body of social legislation was to some extent out of touch with the real conditions of life in Poland, and the claims for sanitary and health provisions in factories were extravagant compared with

[4] Ferdynand Zweig, *Poland between Two Wars* (London: Secker & Warburg, 1944), p. 140.

the general environment. The contrast between the provisions of social legislation for industrial workers and the conditions of work of craftsmen or small peasants was increased by the scope of the social legislation. . . .[5]

As professor of political economy in the University of Cracow, Dr. Zweig had a firsthand experience of the problem; hence his views are extremely valuable.

His final point of a gap between the conditions of the urban workman and the peasant is supported by another important authority. Wilbert E. Moore points up the difference between legal protection and actual protection when he writes:

[Although] all farm labor in Poland was governed by collective agreements, this was only nominally true. These agreements applied most directly to employers and employees on large estates; how extensively they were applied to other workers in the appropriate region covered by the agreements depended partly on the effectiveness of organization among other workers.[6]

In spite of the gap between principle and practice, in spite of an excessive bureaucracy, it seems, nevertheless, fair to give successive Polish ministries in this period credit for having tried very hard to safeguard the worker's interests. Even more would have been achieved in the years immediately preceding 1939 if it had not been for the excessive burdens placed on the Polish economy by the rise of Hitler. Then came total destruction and slavery. As the German mayor of Lodz observed: "On the German soil, reconquered by the gallant German soldiers, there can be but masters and servants—and we are the masters. The Poles must be perfectly clear on that point. . . ."[7] It was

[5] *Ibid.*, pp. 143–144.

[6] Wilbert E. Moore, *Economic Demography of Eastern and Southern Europe* (Geneva: League of Nations, 1945), pp. 225–226.

[7] Speech at Ozorkow, reported in *Litzmannstädter Zeitung*, Sept. 23, 1941.

a pity that someone did not recall on that occasion Robert Browning's grammarian:

> That low man seeks a little thing to do,
> > Sees it and does it:
> This high man, with a great thing to pursue,
> > Dies ere he knows it.

That must be the epitaph on Polish progress in social legislation from 1919 to 1939.

CHAPTER 11

The Balance Sheet,
1919 to 1939

THE PRECEDING chapters have discussed the main structure, sector by sector, of the Polish economy from 1919 to 1939, have set it against its historical background, outlined the main problems, and indicated and to some extent assessed the solutions which were adopted. It seems, therefore, appropriate at this point to try and strike a balance sheet over the whole period for the Polish economy as an organic whole and by setting out the debits and credits to attempt an objective assessment of the achievement of the Polish government and people in the years between the wars. The period from 1919 to 1939 is in itself naturally complete and self-contained, since, at its beginning, it starts with a new state, reborn after an enforced disappearance from the map and history of Europe for some 125 years, while, at the end, we find that new state again wiped off the map of Europe by a fourth partition, enforced upon it this time by Germany and Russia, the same predominant partners in aggression who had destroyed the old Poland at the end of the eighteenth century.

The effects in the economic sphere of the fourth partition of 1939 and of the fifth partition of 1945 will be discussed in the next two chapters, for it was still another Poland which came into being in 1945—one which had lost important territories of the Poland of 1919–1939 to Soviet Russia, and which, at the same time, had gained areas of greater economic importance from Germany. It was also a Poland which, after an uneasy breathing space, was finally swallowed up, economically, if not politically and ideologically, by Soviet Russia. Whether Stalin's Russia can digest Poland any more satisfactorily or permanently than could Czarist Russia is not yet a closed question. As General Bor-Komorowski observes: "To construct world peace at the expense of injustice and wrong done to smaller nations is a dangerous experiment. It can only result in acute political tensions and a perpetual smouldering of grievances—a most precarious state of international affairs, so clearly demonstrated by our present times." [1] This is not the place to consider the possibilities of re-establishing a free Poland once more. It is relevant to our theme, however, to note that Poland after 1945 is not a continuation or projection of the Poland of 1919 to 1939, but a new creation. Before we consider the problems and developments of the economy of Poland under Nazi and Soviet occupation and domination, it is logically appropriate, therefore, to sum up the achievements of the period between the wars.

When we consider the economic prospects which faced the Polish republic in the years immediately after 1919, it is hard to imagine a more difficult task which could have been set for a new state by the workings of history. It was not merely that the new state had to repair the ravages of six years of bitter fighting, during which hostile armies had ranged back and forth across its territories, bringing with them the customary camp followers of devastation, starvation, and disease. To put right the economic ravages of these war years alone would have been a major economic undertaking for any well-established and

[1] T. Bor-Komorowski, *The Secret Army* (New York: The Macmillan Company, 1951).

well-developed state. The new Poland had, however, inherited from the past no solid economic foundation on which to build. For some 125 years, it had been a country only in the hearts and minds of its people. It had had neither geographical nor political existence; its territory had been dismembered by its three powerful neighbors and the parts had been incorporated in three alien countries hostile to one another. Its unity had been destroyed so that what should have developed as an economic whole had been split artificially into three separate parts, each one of which was frontier territory to the absorbing powers.

The evil economic effects of this state of affairs have been briefly described in Chapters 1 and 2. During this long period, no regard was paid to the normal economic development of the Polish lands as an organic whole. In place of what might have been expected if Polish history had run its course smoothly and without interruption from the end of the eighteenth century to the twentieth century, the economic development of the country had been twisted, retarded, and distorted, without any regard to the interests of the Polish people in order that the purely predatory and selfish ends of the three partitioning powers might be served.

When the new state came into being in 1919, therefore, it was faced with an economic prospect which was considerably worse than merely having to start from scratch—it was faced with the hideous damages of war and at the same time with such industries, communications, and market relations as did exist being completely unsuited to the needs of the country. It had to repair immediate damage, but—even more important—it had to undo the evil effects of the period of partition—and, in a country which, although it had certain valuable natural assets, could not by any means be described as a country rich in natural resources, that was no small undertaking. It is particularly important to remember the historical legacies of partition when assessing the accomplishment of Poland over the period from

1919 to 1939 since, otherwise, there is danger of glibly making uncharitable judgments. Very often, when we examine some aspect of Polish economic policy in respect to which a wise decision does not seem to have been taken, for example, the consistent overvaluation of the zloty from 1925 onward, we find that the problem was more complicated than would appear at first sight because of the historical legacy and that a simple application of tests which would be appropriate to, say, Britain, France, or the U.S.A., could not be applied to Poland without danger of faulty judgment. Unfortunately for Poland, only too often in these twenty years, it was a case of what was practicable being the enemy of what was desirable—and government is above all things the art of the practicable. It is, therefore, by the test of what was practicable rather than by what would have been *in vacuo* desirable that the economic achievements of the Polish government and people in the years between the wars should be assessed.

In the first place, Poland was faced in the years after 1919 by an almost insoluble population problem. The rate of natural increase of the Polish population was the highest among the major countries of Europe (excluding the U.S.S.R.). In the years before 1914, substantial relief had been provided by freedom of emigration, notably to the United States, Canada, and Brazil. The blocking of the channels of international migration after 1919 by changes in the immigration policies of these countries greatly intensified the demographic difficulties of the new republic, inevitable from the rapid growth of population in a technically backward agricultural country which was also underdeveloped industrially. Throughout the whole period, there was thus in Poland a very serious problem of "concealed unemployment." Population growth was constantly running a race with industrial development and agrarian reform in the Poland of 1919 to 1939, and on the ability of industrial development and of agrarian reform to keep ahead of population growth depended not prosperity but the very maintenance of the margin between survival and starvation.

On the other hand, this rapidly expanding population was not entirely a liability. The Polish population throughout the period was basically a young population. Provided that industrial development and agrarian reform could make steady progress, there was always available an adequate labor force and a large and potentially expanding internal market for the products of industry and agriculture. These were long-term and potential benefits, however, whereas "concealed unemployment" was a short-run, actual, and urgent problem which *had* to be solved. In point of fact, it had not been solved by 1939. That fact may be considered a mark against the economic policies of the Polish ministries of this period, but it seems doubtful whether a basic problem of this magnitude could have been solved in such a short time as twenty years. Certainly, every Polish administration in this period showed great energy in attempting to solve it; for example, the long-range plans for a complete overhaul of the national economy, of which the development of the Central Industrial District was the first installment. It is not unreasonable to believe that, if war had not interrupted these developments in 1939, the problem would have been solved completely within the fifteen years of Mr. Kwiatkowski's plans. Failure to eradicate "concealed unemployment" by 1939 cannot be counted very heavily against the successive ministries of the interwar years.

Apart from the over-all problem of general overpopulation, there was the further population problem presented by the rural bias of the Polish population. This again was a critical economic problem and one which had been largely inherited from history. Its seriousness has been shown in Chapter 6 (particularly

143

pages 68 to 77). This problem, again, was one intimately connected with a successful policy of agrarian reform linked with industrial development.

From the basic fact that Poland in 1919 had the population of an industrial country but the economic structure and degree of industrialization of a poverty-stricken agricultural country followed certain limiting factors on *any* economic policy which might be undertaken. These factors, which automatically gave a form to economic policy and set the pace of progress, were:

(1) The urgent need for pressing ahead with large-scale plans for industrialization

(2) The urgent need for widespread agrarian reform

(3) The development of the towns as commercial centers and their reintegration with the rest of the national economy

(4) The revival of international trade in order to provide for the necessary imports of essential commodities for the industrialization of the country

(5) The investment problems of a capital-hungry country with a level of domestic savings inadequate to support the economically necessary level of investment

(6) Memories of the severe inflation and currency disorders of the early years of the republic.

Against this general background, let us now attempt to assess, sector by sector, the achievements and shortcomings of the Polish economy in the twenty years from 1919 to 1939. To turn first to the sphere of public finance, banking, and investment, since events in this field affect the whole economy of a country and set the climate, as it were, for developments in the rest of the economic field. The new republic, as we have seen, inherited financial chaos. The establishment of a sound monetary and banking system was the first "must" for the new Poland. On the side of positive achievement, we have the great successes of the Grabski reforms of 1924 and 1925, which resulted in the establishment of a sound and stable currency, the funding of

144

foreign "relief" debts, and the balancing of the national budget. A stable currency, a balanced budget, and the accumulation of Treasury reserves enabled the establishment of an appropriate banking structure on sound and firm foundations to take place and undoubtedly prevented complete economic collapse under the extremely severe strains put on the new economy by the effects of the world economic crisis of the 1930's.

The success of this policy resulted in a great and direct contribution to the alleviation of the acute dearth of capital for investment necessitated by the industrialization of the country. Foreign capital was attracted, and domestic savings were greatly increased—between 1925 and 1928, for example, there was a tenfold increase in deposits in the post office savings bank. The cautious currency policy of successive governments and their prudent policy in regard to raising loans abroad helped substantially in maintaining foreign confidence in Polish currency and credit, an essential prerequisite for ensuring a flow of foreign capital in order to finance industrialization. The basic soundness of this policy and the fundamental healthiness of the new economy may be deduced from the fact that between 1929 and 1935 nearly one-third of the sums advanced by foreign capital were redeemed.

On the debit side in the field of public finance, banking, and investment, two criticisms may be made. In the first place, the maintenance of the circulating media below what objectively was economically desirable had a persistently deflationary effect on economic development. This is a valid criticism, but it should be remembered that the vivid memories of inflation at the birth of the new republic were a political factor which could not be discounted by any prudent government. A government cannot of its own volition carry through the economic policy which it knows to be wise and justifiable by the objective facts —it must have regard to the state of public opinion, since quite apart from the narrowly political considerations involved in governmental decisions under a democracy, any economic policy can be carried through successfully only with the active cooperation of the people. In the light of this limiting factor on governmental economic action, it is a little difficult to see what course other than that actually adopted could have been taken by any Polish government which wished to retain the confidence of the Polish people.

The second charge is a more serious one and rather more difficult to refute—it is that the stabilization of the zloty in 1924 was at too high a level, and though there was a *de facto* devaluation after the happenings of 1925, for the remainder of the period, the zloty was maintained at an exchange level which was not justified by the economic strength of the country. This policy led to severe deflation, to persistent and unnecessary unemployment, to damage to Poland's position in the money markets of the world, and to unnecessary delay in emergence from the depression initially caused by the impact of the world economic crisis on the Polish economy. That these unfortunate events automatically followed upon the currency policies of successive Polish governments in the years after 1925 is undoubtedly true. But, again, we have to look at the financial problem in a wider context. This problem was intimately linked with the problem described in the preceding paragraph. In view of the political and economic necessity of maintaining public confidence in the Polish currency unimpaired, it is doubtful whether *any* Polish government could have successfully followed a policy other than the one which was actually followed.

When we compare the stabilization of the Polish currency in the early 1920's with the experience of other better placed countries such as Germany, the Polish ministries responsible come out of the comparison very favorably. The conclusions of a League of Nations report are worth noting:

The Polish experience is of general interest in that it shows a remarkably close correlation between the budgetary position on the

146

one hand and the exchange value of the currency on the other. . . . In brief, an improvement in the exchange coincided with a determined effort towards budgetary equilibrium. . . .

The way in which this hyper-inflation was brought to an end demonstrates again the paramount importance and the efficacy of fiscal policy. . . .

Altogether it is clear that the chain of causation ran from fiscal reform to exchange stabilization and not the other way round. It should be specially noted that Poland received practically no financial help from abroad in 1924. . . .[2]

The same League of Nations report, moreover, shows considerable sympathy with the view that the second fall of the zloty, in the summer of 1925, can be attributed to temporary and fortuitous causes and not to unsoundness on the part of the Polish government:

Many observers, especially abroad, attributed this unfavorable turn of events to excessive issues of currency notes by the government in the first half of 1925. It is true that the property tax introduced in 1924 failed to bring in the expected amount in 1925, and that the consequent note issues of the government offset the deflationary effect which the sale of foreign exchange by the central bank would otherwise have had, an effect which, in turn, would have tended to correct the disequilibrium in the balance of payments. Yet, having regard to the fact that the principal cause of the disequilibrium— namely, the harvest failure of 1924—was a temporary one, it is plausible to argue, as F. Mlynarski did, that exchange stability could have been maintained if Poland has possessed a monetary reserve adequate to bridge a transitory gap of this sort. "On the eve of a bountiful grain crop and of an equilibrium in the Polish foreign trade balance, the Bank of Poland was at an end of its forces." Based on an analysis of the actual amounts involved, Mlynarski's conclusion was that the stability of the zloty exchange in July 1925 broke down merely "because of a lack of 15 million dollars." The depreciation was compara-

[2] *The Course and Control of Inflation* (League of Nations, 1946), pp. 25–26.

tively moderate; the trade balance recovered; and in 1926 exchange stability was restored. . . .[3]

On balance, therefore, we cannot condemn the Polish governments of this period for certain mistakes in financial policy. On critical occasions, as in 1923/1924, the government in office showed courage and considerable technical skill. Finally, it should not be forgotten that these governments have to their credit the achievements of ultimately establishing a sound currency, with a minimum of external assistance, and of constructing a sound and stable banking structure appropriate to the economic needs of the country. These were not small things to have accomplished.

To turn next to the sphere of agriculture. The facts detailed in Chapters 1, 3, and 6 have given some indication of the major problems facing the new republic in agricultural affairs. The great agrarian reforms which were carried out in this period may be evaluated with the help of the statistics in Table 29 (page 75). We must also count on the credit side the wisdom of the deliberately fostered trend toward mixed farming and the creation of new lines of agricultural exports which has been mentioned in Chapter 7. That they were not pursued with more energy may be largely attributed to the natural poverty of the country. That they did not succeed in providing an adequate standard of living for the peasantry and that they did not solve the problem of "concealed unemployment" in rural areas was not because of any fundamental defect in the policies, but because agrarian action alone could not solve these problems. A successful solution to the Polish agrarian problem depended on the successful industrialization of the country and on the diversification of its economy to redress the imbalance between the agrarian and the industrial sectors. For that major task, twenty years was not a long enough period in which

[3] *The Course and Control of Inflation* (League of Nations, 1946), pp. 60–61.

148

even the most correct policy could hope to achieve success.

In honesty, it must be admitted, however, that land reform was not pushed ahead far enough or quickly enough in the inter-war years. That more could have been achieved was admitted by the Polish government, and it had plans prepared for a more efficient reform to be put into effect after World War II. An official Polish source gave the author the following information in 1944:

Before the war, agricultural reform was carried out under the Agricultural Reform Law issued in 1920 and modified in 1925 and 1930. The progress of agricultural reform was not satisfactory. According to the Law of 1920 the rate of parcellation was not defined. The Law of 1925 defined that 200,000 hectares yearly should be parcelled out. As this rate could not be attained, in 1930 it was diminished to 100,000 hectares yearly. Before the war there were about 4 million hectares left for parcellation.

The Government in London has worked out a new Agricultural Reform Law. This reform will cover 4 million hectares of arable land, which will give occupation to about 1 million persons. . . . The area left to the owner is relatively small, being 50 hectares of arable land. About 200,000 hectares will not be subject to parcellation; this figure is composed of 50,000 hectares designed for exceptionally well managed private agricultural farms and of 150,000 hectares for State and local authorities . . .

The new farms will be one family holdings and their area will be ascertained in such a way as to give full employment to all members of the given family.

In order to assure the effective working of agricultural reform the whole country will be divided into five districts, which will facilitate the adjustment of compensation to the economic conditions of the different parts of a county. The compensation for land, buildings, food plants, and not amortized meliorization investments will be paid in treasury bonds.[4]

[4] *Source:* Extracted from a memorandum to the author from Dr. K. Zaluski of the Economic Department of the Polish Ministry of Industry, Commerce & Shipping, dated Oct. 16, 1944.

The Polish governments of the interwar period may perhaps be censured for not having done more in this field, but the evidence given in Chapter 7 shows that they had achieved a very great deal by 1939, were proceeding on the right lines, and were conscious of their weakness. Developments after 1945 are dealt with in a later chapter.

An assessment of the Polish government's industrial policy is a shade more complicated. On the whole, we may say that the successes of Polish governments in pushing ahead with the industrialization of the country and in diversifying its economy represent a really remarkable achievement when all the difficulties are taken into account. The Polish people and their governments showed not only energy, technical skill, and great capacity for hard work—they also showed great foresight and wisdom in the use of carefully planned state investment in a manner which not merely promoted immediately sound ends within the limits of individual projects but had a noteworthy "multiplier effect" in promoting the parallel advancement and progress of private enterprise. The success of the Central Industrial District and of the development of the port of Gdynia are the most outstanding instances of this general thesis. The success of the policy may be seen from the fact that whereas in 1929 agriculture accounted for 68 per cent of the national output and industry and mining for only 32 per cent, by 1939 industry and mining accounted for over 50 per cent of the total. The steady rise in the index of Polish industrial production between 1932, when it stood at 64.0, and the spring of 1939, when it had risen to 125.8, is a relevant and incontrovertible test. (For details of movements in the index see Table 37, page 91.)

That this policy of encouragement of private enterprise went hand in hand with care for the interest of the ordinary consumer may be judged from the policy of the close control of cartels when they appeared to be acting against the consumer.

On the debit side, we have to take account of Poland's late

emergence from the economic depression of the 1930's and of the persistence of unemployment at a time when the available labor force could have been usefully employed (Table 53, page 130). We have seen, however, that the causes for this phenomenon are to be found in the financial policy of the period, which demanded the maintenance of the zloty at too high an exchange rate, and not in the sphere of industrial policy. In itself, however, the industrial policy which was followed accentuated the foreign exchange difficulties, since the pushing ahead of large-scale plans for industrialization led to the need for a relatively very high volume of essential imports, and this demand put in the end an unbearable strain on the Polish balance of payments.

In regard to the organization of commerce, there were no spectacular achievements similar to those in the fields of agrarian reform and industrialization; there were, however, no spectacular mistakes. The record shows substantial positive achievements, particularly in the sphere of the co-operative movement.

With regard to the search for markets, the Polish government made one big mistake, which has been mentioned already as having had adverse effects on industrial development, and that is that the artificial boom produced by the inflationary conditions of the early years of the new republic, although it needed correcting, was cut off too sharply by Grabski's currency reforms. The consequent overvaluation of the zloty resulted in persistent weaknesses in Poland's position in regard to the balance of international payments, and this undoubtedly hampered the commercial and industrial recovery of the country. Some of these weaknesses, however, as has just been observed, were the inevitable consequences of the need for very high imports of essential raw materials and for industrial plants required for the industrialization of the country. Against this mistake should be set such successes as the development of the great new port of Gdynia and of the Polish merchant marine. The period, moreover, was one of a very considerable and desirable broadening of Polish foreign trade.[5] In spite of such disturbing factors as the tariff war with Germany and the persistent currency difficulties, the progress of Poland's foreign trade over the period and, more particularly, its recovery after the world economic crisis of the early 1930's, represented a very substantial achievement.[6]

When we attempt to assess improvements in the condition of the people over the twenty years from 1919 to 1939, we find that a careful judgment involves a nice balancing of complex facts. In the first place, it is important that we should make full allowance for the natural poverty of the country and for its devastated condition in 1919, the result of several years of war, famine, and disease. The only valid method seems to be to consider improvement over the initial standards at the beginning of the period and to avoid direct comparisons with older, less disturbed, and initially more developed countries. Against such a background, we can point to a steady record of achievement in the Poland of 1919 to 1939.

To claim this much is not to gloss over certain appalling facts which remained true throughout the whole twenty years. In the first place, there was the bad distribution of the national income as between dwellers in urban and rural areas.[7] In spite of the effects of agrarian reforms and of the development of better farming techniques, the condition of the majority of the peasantry throughout the entire period was wretched. In the second place, for many years, there was persistent and heavy industrial unemployment.

Against these black patches may be seen, however, many substantial achievements. Between 1928 and 1936 there was an upward trend in real wages: the peasant's misfortunes were not without their compensations for the industrial worker.[8]

[5] See Table 46, p. 121.
[6] See Table 45, p. 120.
[7] See Table 48, p. 125, and Table 49, p. 126.
[8] See Table 51, p. 128.

There were a reasonable working week, annual holidays with pay, and a comprehensive (indeed, many would consider, an overambitious) system of social security. State public works not only provided employment in themselves, but they were so planned and executed that they stimulated the revival and expansion of private enterprise. On balance, there was very clearly a great improvement in the standard of living of the Polish people during these years.

In their economic activities, the Poles showed energy, enlightenment, foresight, imagination, capacity for hard work, and considerable planning and executive ability. If they had not solved all their problems in twenty years, they were well on the way to solutions when in September, 1939, all these achievements were to be swept away by a double invasion from their traditional foes. Taking into account their evil inheritance in 1919 and also the many adverse factors of the period from 1919 to 1939, we may well feel justified in concluding that, taken all in all, Polish economic achievement in those twenty years was outstanding.

Part III

ECONOMIC DEVELOPMENTS
AFTER 1939

CHAPTER 12

The Polish Economy under Nazi-Soviet Occupation

ON SEPTEMBER 1, 1939, Poland was invaded by the armed forces of the German Reich and was rapidly overrun. Any faint hope of prolonged resistance was definitely dispelled on September 17, 1939, when the armed forces of the Soviet Union invaded Poland from the east and took in the rear the remaining remnants of resistance. Between these two huge millstones, the Polish state could no longer hope to exist. On September 28, 1939, was signed the Ribbentrop-Molotov Agreement which effected the fourth partition of Poland. This time there were only two parties to carve up the corpse, since the Hapsburg empire had long ago disappeared and its successor states had either been absorbed into the German Reich or had been brought completely within its sphere of influence as dutiful satellites.

The two new partitioning powers divided up the loot as shown in Table 54.

Within the German- and Russian-occupied areas, there were vast movements of population. Approximately 1,000,000 Poles were forcibly moved into Russia proper, treading the sad and bitter path of exile with which their fathers and grandfathers

157

TABLE 54. THE FOURTH PARTITION OF POLAND (AS ON JANUARY 1, 1941).*

	Percentage of 1939 population of Poland
German-occupied area	62.7
Soviet-occupied area	37.3
German area:	
Annexed into the Reich	30.0
Government-General of Poland	32.6
Slovakia	0.1
Russian area:	
Lithuania	1.5
White Ruthenia	13.4
Ukraine	22.4

* Source: Extracted from *Concise Statistical Year-Book of Poland, 1939–41*, p. 5, table 11.

had been so painfully familiar. There were also forcible evictions from the Polish area absorbed into the German Reich to the area of the Government-General, and there was in addition a directed movement of Germans into the former Polish territories. The Baltic Germans, for example, received about 3,000 industrial properties, more than 2,500 agricultural properties, and more than 2,000 workshops. To run confiscated industrial establishments in Lodz alone, more than 3,000 German officials were brought into the area. The emigration of German businessmen to Poland was encouraged by preferential taxes, by special subsidies, and by the provision of special credit facilities. Moreover, the Reich's commissar of prices pegged the price levels in the Reich proper in order to make settlement in the former Polish territories more attractive to Germans.

Although it is in a sense ancient history now, it is perhaps worth looking briefly, sector by sector, at the main points in the economic development of Poland under Nazi-Soviet occupation, since it left legacies which will have to be dealt with by the new post-1945 Poland. Under the German occupation, Polish banking was virtually destroyed. The reichsmark was very heavily overvalued as against the zloty, and, since the Nazi authorities rigidly controlled prices, an inducement was created for Germans to go to Poland and to strip the country of all available commodities at absurdly low prices. In the area of the Government General, a bank of issue was created which started out entirely devoid of gold reserves. Its notes were covered by its discount transactions and by its holdings of German marks. The zloty had to be exchanged against the new bank notes, which became the only legal tender.

No returns regarding the position of commercial banks were published after 1939. No detailed returns or balance sheets were published for the "Bank of Issue in Poland." Table 55 shows about all the information that is available. The rapid increase in notes in circulation is one indication of the inflationary effect of the German occupation.

TABLE 55. "BANK OF ISSUE IN POLAND." *

	1941 (end)	1942 (end)	1944 (June)
Assets (in billion zloty):			
Debt of the occupying authorities	1.4	3.1	
Notes of the Bank of Poland (withdrawn from circulation)	2.0	2.0	
Liabilities (in billion zloty):			
Notes in circulation	2.3	4.2	7.5
Current accounts	1.3	1.2	—

*Source: Money and Banking, 1942/44 (Geneva: League of Nations, 1945), p. 167.

159

Like the other occupied countries, Poland was compelled to contribute to the demoralization of its own currency and credit system by making forced loans to Germany. The three methods used were:

(1) the acquisition of German government paper by the central and commercial banks,

(2) a growing adverse clearing balance owed by Germany which the German Clearing Office invested in German government loans,

(3) the issue of "occupation marks." The wrecking of the Polish currency and credit system was very effective.

With the division of the country into three parts as a result of German and Russian policy after the Ribbentrop-Molotov Agreement, the economic equilibrium, toward which successive Polish governments had so painfully and not unsuccessfully worked over a period of twenty years, was destroyed. The area of the Government-General could never be self-sufficient if its inhabitants were to have even a minimum subsistence standard of living. The parts of Poland annexed to the Reich proper were destined by the Nazis to become the granary of the Greater Germany, and after their incorporation into the Reich the Nazi government insisted on a large export of agricultural produce from them into the other parts of Germany. One consequence of this policy was that agriculture in western Poland suffered less than in the other parts of the country since it was in Germany's own interest to keep it efficient and in good shape. In order to achieve a higher yield per unit acre, the Nazis endeavored to increase the use of artificial fertilizers and of tractors and tractor-drawn implements. German settlers in the incorporated provinces were given special courses in mechanized methods of agriculture.

With regard to the agricultural development of the Government-General, the Nazis outlined ambitious plans, but how far they were more than ingenious methods of exploiting the soil to give maximum yields for a short period, irrespective of long-term consequences in the form of soil exhaustion and erosion, cannot be determined with any accuracy. The Nazis followed a policy of devastation of Polish forests by unlimited exploitation, however, so it is not unreasonable to assume that their policy in respect to other sectors of the Polish agricultural economy was also purely predatory. In eastern Poland, there was much greater devastation of agriculture than in the western provinces for the simple reason that eastern Poland was the front line in June, 1941, when Germany invaded the territories of its former accomplice in aggression.

It was estimated in March, 1943, that the average losses of Polish agriculture to that date were as follows:

TABLE 56. DEVASTATION OF POLISH AGRICULTURE (1939–1943).

	Percentage decrease on prewar
Area under grain (excluding rye)	30
Yield of cereals per acre	20
Pig population	20
Cattle	35
Horses	40
Sheep	30

It is difficult, if not impossible, to give accurate figures for the devastation of Poland from 1939 to 1945 because the end of the war was marked by changes in the territory of Poland, and this complicates the calculation. Figures for a comparison between the resources of the new Poland in 1945 and of the old Poland of pre-1939 are given, however, in the next chapter, to which they are more relevant. The big estates of western and central Poland suffered far less than the small peasant holdings, but it is important to remember that 89 per cent of Polish agricultural holdings before the war were small peasant holdings of less than ten hectares each. As a generalization, it is fair to say that

161

despite all German attempts to turn Poland into the granary of the Reich, the level of agricultural production under the German occupation sank to a primitive standard. In 1941, the whole of Russian-occupied Poland was overrun by the Nazis when they invaded Soviet Russia.

One indirect way of making an estimate of the damage done to Polish agriculture is by examining the food consumption levels, and, fortunately, there is a certain amount of reliable evidence on this point compiled by the League of Nations and by the United Nations Relief and Rehabilitation Administration. In general, Poland suffered more than any other European country except Greece, parts of Yugoslavia, and German-occupied Russia (which, of course, included that part of prewar Poland that had been seized by the U.S.S.R.). As we shall see later, moreover, such food as was available was unevenly distributed —so that general average figures of food consumption are more than usually misleading. The low level of productivity in agriculture became worse after 1942 for a number of reasons. The main ones were the exceptionally severe and protracted winter of 1941/1942, shortages of farm labor, shortages of draft animals, and shortages of fertilizer. For a country like Poland, which had had a very low standard before the war, this was disastrous, particularly since there were no black market additions of any substance to mitigate official supplies, as there were in France and Italy. The general position was summed up in a League of Nations report as follows: "In Poland, Greece, parts of Yugoslavia and Albania distribution was irregular and consumption fell for shorter or longer periods to levels of semi-starvation or outright famine." [1]

The severe drop in food consumption in Poland and its rapid deterioration after 1942 may be seen from Table 57.

To get some understanding of the figures, it is interesting to compare them with the per capita calorie intake of the civilian

[1] *Food, Famine and Relief* (Geneva: League of Nations, 1946), p. 5.

162

TABLE 57. FOOD CONSUMPTION IN CALORIES PER CONSUMPTION UNIT
OF A TYPICAL FAMILY IN POLAND (GOVERNMENT-GENERAL
AREA) (PREWAR AND 1941–1944).*

Food	1929	1941	1942	1943	1944
Bread and Flour	1,550	690	705	820	840
Cereals	100	70	90	45	50
Potatoes	445	490	415	330	345
Sugar, jam, etc.	215	175	165	115	115
Meat and meat products	335	60	45	55	55
Fish	5	—	—	—	—
Fats	120	130	90	—	—
Whole milk	140	135	125	—	—
Skimmed milk	5	—	—	—	—
Cream	20	—	—	—	—
Cheese	15	25	25	—	—
Eggs	15	55	—	—	—
Fresh vegetables	50	—	—	—	—
Fresh fruits	10	—	—	—	—
Totals	3,025	1,830	1,650	1,365	1,405

* Source: Food, Famine and Relief (Geneva: League of Nations, 1946),
p. 36.

population in the United States, Canada, and Great Britain in
1943, which were as follows: [2]

	Calories per person per day	Percentage change, 1943 and prewar
United States	3,283	+2
Canada	3,223	+3
United Kingdom	2,827	−5

These general figures for Poland do not fully represent the
seriousness of the situation in some areas and for some groups of

[2] Extracted from Food Consumption Levels in the United States, Canada,
and the United Kingdom (H. M. Stationery Office, 1944), p. 19, table.

163

the population—they give the official rations which it was not always possible to honor and of which some groups were deprived:

> In considering the situation in Poland and Yugoslavia, the predominantly agrarian nature of these countries must be taken into account. Official rations in Poland represented perhaps some 50% of requirements and may have been accessible to Poles in the provinces "incorporated" with Germany (Germans received the German rations); but it is not possible to make a generalization on the basis of conditions in the "Government General." Rations were less generally available, and the authorities were often obliged—in order to maintain the working efficiency of labour employed in industries considered as essential—to have recourse to canteen feeding. The insufficiency and irregularity of rationing compelled city dwellers to have recourse to the black market in order to survive; but as prices soared out of their reach, ordinary wage-earners became subject to great privations. The rations of Jews amounted to half of the insufficient rations granted to Poles; and when the Jews were officially considered exterminated, no further issues of rationing cards were made to them.[3]

The devastating effects of this inadequate diet were shown in a debilitated population, apart, of course, from actual deaths caused by near-starvation and famine. It is difficult to measure statistically the prevalence of specific deficiency diseases. Typhus and typhoid fever increased alarmingly, while, as might have been expected, rickets, scurvy, gastrointestinal troubles, and hunger oedema increased. There was thus a qualitative as well as a quantitative population loss, a not unimportant fact when considering the prospects of economic growth.

The division of German-occupied Poland was made on economic lines. The more fertile and better-cultivated agricultural areas were incorporated directly into the Greater Reich, while the economically preposterous rump was made into the Government-General, a *nebenland,* or area of exploitation, of

[3] *Food, Famine and Relief* (Geneva: League of Nations, 1936), p. 39.

the Greater Reich. German economic policy thus had different aims in the two areas. The areas occupied by the U.S.S.R. in 1939 were incorporated in the Government-General in August, 1941, and were then made subject to the same policy as prevailed earlier in that area. In the incorporated area, the aim was the grafting of the former Polish economy on to the economy of the Reich so that it would be completely absorbed, economically, as well as politically, into Germany. The indigenous Polish population—87.2 per cent of the total population of the area—was to be removed and replaced by Germans. Thus Hitler planned to carry out once and for all the policy which Bismarck had tried but had failed to accomplish in the latter part of the nineteenth century. Some 1,500,000 Poles out of the 9,000,000 normally inhabiting the region were actually deported, but the magnitude of the task and the lack of enthusiasm on the part of German immigrants into the area led to a slowing down of the process by the beginning of 1941. Deprived of their property and expropriated without compensation from their industrial enterprises, the Poles were allowed to provide cheap labor to keep the existing industries going or were transported into the interior of Germany for forced labor.

While the complete elimination of Poles and Jews was the aim of the German government in respect to the incorporated provinces, its aim in the Government-General was agricultural specialization combined with unrestricted economic exploitation. The area was to be deindustrialized and turned over to the supply of agricultural commodities and raw materials. The policy of dismantling factories and of transporting their equipment to Germany was reversed, however, in 1940 and 1941, under the stress of the wartime economic needs of the Nazi military machine. Efforts were made to increase the output of oil and iron and to develop the armaments industries of the Central Industrial District. These industries were linked with the *Hermann Goering Werke*, while early in 1940 Goering set up the *Haupttreuhandstelle Ost* for the purpose of extending his four-year

165

plan to the eastern areas of the Reich to which the territory of the Government-General must be consided as belonging from the economic point of view. By means of Goering's organization, the Nazis confiscated all the economically important industries of the region, for example, coal mines, the oil industry, the beet sugar industry, and more than 80 per cent of the chemical industry. All factories in the area of the Government-General which had been Polish state property were united in *Die Werke des General Gouvernement A.G.*, an organization on the lines of the *Hermann Goering Werke*. Steps were then taken to obtain financial control of the remaining Polish industries, and this control, once obtained, was used to make drastic changes. The less efficient plants were closed down, and their machinery was dismantled and transferred to other parts of the Reich. The more efficient establishments were enlarged, new machinery was installed, and production was concentrated in them. Needless to say, the former Polish owners were expropriated without compensation.

In June, 1941, the armed forces of the German Reich invaded Russian territory, thus bringing the fourth partition of Poland to an end. From 1941 to the end of the war, the Polish territories which had hitherto been divided between Nazi Germany and Soviet Russia were completely absorbed into the territory of the Reich. From the economic point of view, the whole period from the end of 1939 to the middle of 1945 is best considered as an interlude characterized by the ruthless exploitation for non-Polish purposes of the Polish economy.

Apart from the unusually severe devastation of economic resources, the Polish economy suffered in common from the consequences of the German "new order" for Europe. These have been summarized as follows:

The "New Order" programme which Germany launched in 1940 had as one of its objectives the integration of the European economy. . . .

The actual tendency after 1942 was exactly the opposite: the transport situation, which was steadily deteriorating, led to a progressive disintegration of the economy of German-occupied Europe. . . . The German authorities were thus driven to adopt a policy deliberately designed to split the continent into more or less self-sufficient trade areas. . . .

The transport problem was responsible also for aggravating the food shortages in the cities of the occupied and satellite countries, even when farmers in the countryside had surplus food. . . .

Besides production and transport difficulties, there was yet another general factor tending to reduce the urban food supply, and that was the reluctance of farmers to sell their products. This reluctance was due in varying degrees to the farmers' inability to buy anything useful with the money received; expectations of price increases for the products concerned; and unwillingness to support the German war economy. . . . The control of farm deliveries was one of the most stubborn economic difficulties the Germans encountered. . . .[4]

In short, the Polish economy at the end of the second World War was left in as bad a state—if not worse—as at the end of the first World War. It seemed that the great constructive economic achievements of the period between the wars had been in vain.

[4] *World Economic Survey, 1942/44* (Geneva: League of Nations, 1945), pp. 30–31.

CHAPTER 13

The Polish Economy
after the Fifth Partition

ALLIED victory in 1945 did not bring about a restoration of
Poland to its prewar territories. After the German invasion of
Russia in June, 1941, the Soviet government and the Polish
government-in-exile, located in London, entered into an agreement in the July of that year declaring null and void the German-
Soviet agreements effected after September 1, 1939. This agreement was followed in December, 1941, by a Polish-Soviet Declaration of Friendship and Mutual Assistance. It seemed,
therefore, that the fourth partition of Poland had been nullified
and that the way was clear for the restoration of Poland to its prewar territories after the ultimate victory of the Allied Powers
over the Nazi aggressors.

Things were not, however, to work out that way. In July, 1944,
a Polish Committee of National Liberation, set up in eastern
Poland and completely under Communist domination, was recognized by the Soviet government. There thus came into being
two Polish governments—the lawful government-in-exile in
London, recognized by all the allied powers up to this time, and
the Communist committee in Lublin controlled by Soviet Russia,
having no legal status but being in effective control of the
country.

168

In February, 1945, there took place the Yalta Conference between President Franklin D. Roosevelt, Prime Minister Winston S. Churchill, and Premier Joseph Stalin. The author is not particularly expert in diplomatic history and would not venture to make a general appraisal of the very controversial decisions taken at that conference. There may have been good reasons— doubtless, there were—for the complicated horse trading that took place. Here, it is relevant to note that one part of the deal was a fifth partition of Poland. General Bor-Komorowski sums up the position in these words:

The Western powers, in their eagerness to settle down to a peaceful existence, let themselves be led astray by the hope of Soviet Russia's cooperation in a political and economic reconstruction of the world. This wishful thinking was followed by a policy of concessions to Stalin, with the result that central-eastern Europe passed under Communist domination. Poland was one of the victims.[1]

It is interesting to note that this fifth partition of Poland was carried through without consultation with the legal Polish government. A few days before the Yalta Conference, the Polish government had addressed a memorandum to the British and American governments in which it stated:

The Polish Government are of the opinion that territorial questions should be settled after the termination of hostilities. In this matter, the opinion of the Polish Government coincides with the general principles enunciated by the Governments of Great Britain and the United States of America.

The Polish Government are prepared for a friendly settlement of the Polish-Soviet dispute, arising from the claims of the USSR to the Eastern territories of the Polish Republic, and they will agree to any method provided for by international law for a just and equitable settlement of the dispute, with the participation of both sides.

Furthermore, the Polish Government are determined to conclude

[1] T. Bor-Komorowski, *The Secret Army* (New York: The Macmillan Co., 1951).

with the USSR an alliance guaranteeing the security of both States, and to collaborate closely with the Government of the USSR within a framework of a universal international security organization and within that of an economic organization of the States of Central-Eastern Europe. However . . . the Polish Government cannot be expected to recognise decisions unilaterally arrived at.

The Polish Government are confident that the Government of Great Britain will not agree to be a party to decisions concerning the Allied Polish Republic arrived at without the participation and consent of the Polish Government. The Polish Government confidently trust that at the conference of the Great Allied Powers, the British Government will give expression to their resolve not to recognise a puppet government. The recognition of such a "government" in Poland would be tantamount to the recognition of the abolition of the independence of Poland, in defence of which the present war was begun.[2]

The Polish confidence in good faith among allies was disappointed, and, without either the participation, authorization, or knowledge of the Polish government, the "Big Three" made their own arrangements for disposing of the territories of an allied power still fighting the common enemy. The Polish government made a dignified protest immediately after the Yalta decision was communicated to it in which it stated:

The method adopted in the case of Poland is a contradiction of the elementary principles binding the Allies and constitutes a violation of the letter and spirit of the Atlantic Charter and the right of every nation to defend its own interests.

The Polish Government declares that the decisions of the Three Power Conference concerning Poland cannot be recognised by the Polish Government and cannot bind the Polish Nation.

The Polish Nation will consider the severance of the Eastern half of the territory of Poland through the imposition of a Polish-Soviet frontier following the so-called Curzon Line as a fifth partition of Poland now accomplished by her Allies. The intention of the Three

[2] *Memorandum Handed to the British and American Governments on January 22nd, 1945.*

170

Powers to create a "provisional Polish Government of National Unity" by enlarging the foreign appointed Lublin Committee with persons vaguely described as "democratic leaders from Poland itself and Poles abroad," can only legalise Soviet interference in Polish internal affairs. As long as the territory of Poland will remain under the sole occupation of Soviet troops, a Government of that kind will not safeguard to the Polish nation even in the presence of British and American diplomats the unfettered rights of free expression. . . .

It was too late, however, for such remonstrations to have any effect—the job [3] had been done. The future was to demonstrate the truth of the forebodings in the last part of the protest.

After much diplomatic jockeying, a Polish Government of National Unity was formed in June, 1945, by the amalgamation of some members of the government-in-exile with the Committee of National Liberation in Lublin. On July 5, 1945, this new government was recognized by the governments of Britain and of the U.S.A. Previous to this—in April, 1945—a treaty of friendship, mutual assistance, and postwar collaboration had been signed between the Lublin Committee of National Liberation and the Soviet government.

The postwar settlements of August, 1945, brought Poland back into existence as an internationally recognized state, but it was a different Poland from that of 1919 to 1939. It had lost territories in the east to Russia but had gained economically more valuable territories in the west at the expense of Germany. The eastern frontier of Poland was fixed roughly along the so-called Curzon Line, and the Soviet gains from Poland took in not merely what had been admittedly disputed territory between the Poles and the Ukrainians but, in addition, much territory that was indubitably Polish, such as the area of Lwów and its surroundings. A slight rectification of this eastern frontier was

[3] A "job" in the best eighteenth-century, as well as modern, sense. The shades of Frederick and of Maria Theresa must have had a ghostly chuckle on the theme *plus ça change, plus c'est la même chose.*

171

made on August 16, 1945, when the new Polish government and the Soviet Union signed a treaty delimiting the Polish-Soviet frontier. By this treaty, the U.S.S.R. ceded to Poland two small areas east of the Curzon Line but maintained its annexation of Lwów and other Polish territories.

On August 2, 1945, at Potsdam, Attlee, Truman, and Stalin had previously established a new *de facto* western frontier for Poland along the Oder-Neisse line, pending the final peace treaty. It seems that this provisional line will be the definitive western frontier of the new Poland unless the Soviet Union decides that some of the former German territory at present under Polish administration must be handed back to Germany as part of Russia's attempts to create a Soviet state in Germany. The Polish government itself [4] has repeatedly stated, moreover, that it regards this western frontier, incorporating in Poland former eastern territories of Germany, as inviolable. The upshot of these agreements between Poland, Soviet Russia, Britain, and the U.S.A. was that Poland was, as it were, bodily shifted westward. The over-all figures for population and territorial change are given in Table 58.

TABLE 58. POPULATION AND TERRITORIAL CHANGES
(PREWAR AND POSTWAR).*

	Prewar	Postwar	Loss
Population (thousands)	34,359	23,970	10,389
Area (thousand sq. km.)	389.7	311.7	78.0

* *Sources:* For postwar figures and prewar population, *Statistical Year-book* (United Nations, 1950), p. 25; for prewar area, *Concise Statistical Year-Book of Poland, 1939–41.*

The over-all figures, however, are misleading in that the shifting westward of Poland had important economic advantages. The

[4] For the rest of this chapter the term "Polish government" refers to the *de facto* government in Poland and not to the London government or its successors.

territories lost to Russia were, except for the Lwów area, rather poor agricultural land. The area gained from Germany between the prewar Polish-German border and the Neisse and Oder rivers is, for the most part, good agricultural land and contains an important industrial area. It also includes the bituminous and anthracite coal deposits of both Upper and Lower Silesia. A further important economic gain is the disappearance of the prewar Polish Corridor, involving an extension of the Polish coast line so that postwar Poland has, in addition to the port of Gdynia, the ports of Danzig and Szczecin (Stettin). The Oder, moreover, makes an important addition to the Vistula from the point of view of inland navigation. Economically, therefore, the territorial changes of the postwar settlement, no matter how reprehensible the manner in which they were brought about, were to the advantage of Poland.

Before we consider in detail the economic developments in Poland since 1945, we should note the economic significance of the territorial changes embodied in the fifth partition. In brief, those changes meant that Poland remained essentially an agricultural country, while gaining important industrial areas which will make more easy of achievement the attainment of a better-balanced economy.

The German lands in the west, which have now been incorporated into Poland, accounted before World War II for about 25 per cent of Germany's food production. About 55 per cent of the new Poland is arable land; the corresponding figure prewar was 49 per cent. Farming conditions continued to be disturbed throughout 1945, 1946, and 1947. One consequence was that the Polish peasants continued to live on a bare subsistence basis throughout these years, while the greatly reduced urban population subsisted near the lower margin of mere brute existence.

We can get some idea of the devastation wrought during the war years on Polish agriculture from the fact that if we take the period 1934 to 1938 as a base with an agricultural production of 100, then for the year 1945/1946 the level of agricultural production for Poland was 33, while for the year 1946/1947 it had risen to only 45. The Food and Agriculture Organization of the United Nations sent a mission to Poland in the summer of 1947. The mission reported that improved agricultural techniques could increase Polish productivity well above prewar levels. It said, however, that the achievement of this goal would "depend on permanent adoption of policies and practices widely at variance with some of those which have been traditional in Poland and equally at variance with some that have been recently devised." Although the Polish government has hitherto co-operated with the Food and Agriculture Organization of the United Nations, it seems unlikely that any economic recommendations at variance with the social policies of the Communist-dominated government, no matter how necessary they may be on purely economic grounds, will be adopted.

The achievements of the Polish administration in respect to agriculture in the years after 1945 must not, however, be underestimated because of one's political dislike of the regime. Even before the end of hostilities the Lublin committee proclaimed sweeping land reforms. Agrarian land was dealt with in the decree of the Polish National Liberation Committee of September 6, 1944, and in the decree of August 8, 1946. The nationalization of forests was announced in the decree of December 12, 1944. According to official information,[5] the arrangements set up were as follows:

Regulations dealing with land reform provide for the creation of a National Land Fund . . . under the administration of the Ministry of Agriculture and Land Reforms. Lands surrendered under this scheme are dependent upon this fund, and comprise land owned by the Treasury, former German landed property, landed property of

[5] This paragraph is based upon material supplied me by the Polish Research and Information Service, New York. I am solely responsible, however, for the interpretation as distinct from factual matter.

persons sentenced for treason, desertion or collaboration, confiscated landed property and, in general, all landed property exceeding 124 acres of arable land (in some cases 247 acres), and in the provinces of Poznan, Silesia and Pomerania, landed property exceeding 247 acres.

This Decree does not apply to land owned by religious communities; such land will be disposed of by the Legislative Assembly, nor property divided prior to September 1, 1939, into portions smaller than those stated above. . . .

It is interesting to compare with this the plans of the London government, which proposed to bring about reforms which would cover about 4,000,000 hectares, leaving normally a maximum of only 50 hectares in the hands of the original owners, except for exceptionally well-managed private farms.

The decree of September, 1944, provided:

All the aforementioned lands are to be taken over immediately, together with their chattels, for the purposes defined by the land reform scheme and will be administered by the Ministry of Agriculture and Land Reforms. For this purpose, the Minister appoints deputies for the provinces who, in cooperation with the local farm committees, prepare lists of the properties concerned and chattels involved, provide for their safekeeping, and arrange for the eviction of the previous owners. Land thus transferred will be divided into self-supporting farms, averaging 12 acres each, except those lands which totally or in part are restricted and set aside for the expansion of cities, schools, experimental farms for the development of higher standards of cultivation, cattle-breeding, seed growing or vegetable allotments in city areas, land destined for partial industrialization, or by-pass road schemes.

As compared with the proposals of the London government, the plans of the Lublin committee may be criticized as being unrealistic in the sense that the units which would result were too small for efficient agricultural practices. Economic advantage seems to have been sacrificed to political expediency. That the

175

land reforms were overhasty and not altogether too wisely planned from an economic point of view helps to explain why the development of agriculture in postwar Poland has lagged behind industrial development.

One important difference, as might be expected, between the land reform plans of the London government and those of the *de facto* Lublin government was in respect to compensation. The London government would have been more equitable to the dispossessed owners by compensating them at reasonable market value and making the cost a charge on the public debt (rather like the nationalization arrangements of the British Labor government). The decree of September, 1944, provided: "The dispossessed former owners of estates, may be allotted a farmhold or will be granted as compensation the salary of a Category VI government official. . . ." Although these arrangements seem harsh and perhaps immoral to anyone with the traditional Western regard for the sanctity of property rights, it is important to remember the prewar agrarian misery of the representative Polish peasant. Such expropriation may not perhaps be excused, but it can readily be understood. The more serious criticism of these reforms is that they went too far in parcellation and resulted in agrarian units below efficient size.

The criticisms of the postwar land reforms which were made by some students of the subject in the years immediately after the war, however, may well have been premature. It is true that agrarian developments have lagged behind industrial progress, but, considered by themselves, the achievements have been very great. By 1948, for example, the uncultivated area of arable land had declined from 48.2 per cent of the total in 1945 to less than 10 per cent. The precise figures are given in Table 59.

At the same time, decline in yield per hectare, which was particularly noticeable in the immediate postwar years and which may have been partially caused by the haste of land reform, had slightly surpassed the prewar levels by 1948. By the

TABLE 59. DECLINE IN UNCULTIVATED ARABLE LAND IN HECTARES
(1945–1948).*

1945	7,941,000
1946	5,958,000
1947	2,497,000
1948	1,480,000

* *Source:* Figures taken from Hilary Minc, *Poland's Economy: Present and Future* (New York: Polish Research and Information Service, 1949), p. 6.

end of 1949, the actual area sown to crops was almost equal to, or had slightly surpassed, the prewar level. The figures are shown in Table 60.

TABLE 60. AREA SOWN FOR CROPS (1938 AND 1949).*

Crop	1938	1949
	Thousand hectares	*Thousand hectares*
Rye	5,352.1	5,025.0
Potatoes	2,756.3	2,500.0
Oats	1,951.9	1,750.0
Wheat	1,343.1	1,450.0
Barley	1,040.3	1,040.0
Sugar beets	225.0	233.0

* *Source:* Figures taken from *Poland Today*, 5 (Feb., 1950), 4.

In livestock production, the story is not quite so encouraging, but this sector of agriculture had been particularly hard hit by wartime devastation. In 1945, the horse population was only 35.6 per cent of prewar; cattle, 31.5; hogs, 22.6; and sheep, 20.7. The restoration of a livestock population so severely depleted is a slow process—nature cannot be hurried in this matter— hence, while all other foodstuffs had been taken off ration by December, 1949, meat (except poultry) remained subject to rationing.

177

The general level of food consumption, however, in spite of the very great progress in restoring agricultural production remained below a satisfactory nutritional level. The *prewar* figures for the United States and the United Kingdom are shown in Table 61.

TABLE 61. PREWAR SUPPLY OF NUTRIENTS PER PERSON, U.S.A. AND UNITED KINGDOM.*

	U.S.A.	U.K.
Calories	3,228	2,984
Proteins (grams)	89	81
Fats (grams)	132	130

* Source: *Food Consumption Levels,* Report of a Special Joint Committee Set up by the Combined Food Board, H.M.S.O. (London, 1944), p. 16.

With these figures may be compared the postwar Polish figures (Table 62).

TABLE 62. SUPPLY OF NUTRIENTS PER PERSON, POLAND (1945–1948).*

Domestic Production	Calories †	Proteins (*grams*)	Fats (*grams*)
1945–1946	1,375	35	21
1946–1947	1,723	45	27
1947–1948	1,882	48	36
Deliveries from abroad			
1945–1946	327	11	8
1946–1947	251	9	5
1947–1948	280	9	7
Totals			
1945–1946	1,702	46	29
1946–1947	1,974	54	32
1947–1948	2,162	57	42

* Source: *Poland Today,* 3, (Oct., 1948), 7.
† Does not include fresh-water fish, fruits, and some vegetables.

178

Nevertheless, when compared with the prewar Polish position, these relatively low figures are an improvement. The better-off members of the population in the urban areas may have suffered, but the bulk of the rural population almost certainly have a better supply of food than they did in prewar times. It is one of the major concerns of the administration to bring nutritional levels up to reasonable adequacy when compared with countries such as the United States and the United Kingdom.

Specific government aid to agriculture and the role allotted to the agrarian sector in a planned economy will be considered later in this chapter in connection with the Three-Year Plan and the Six-Year Plan.

The industrial resources of Poland, as might have been expected from the facts given in the previous chapter, were severely damaged by the events of World War II, but they were not greatly affected by the territorial concessions to the U.S.S.R. with the exception of the loss of the industrial resources of the Lwów area. On the other hand, important industrial areas located in former German territory, especially in Silesia and around Stettin, were placed under Polish control. In many ways, indeed, the territorial changes increased Poland's industrial resources. The principal gains are shown in Table 63, which is based on information in the U.N.R.R.A. paper, "Industrial Rehabilitation in Poland."

TABLE 63. POLAND'S INDUSTRIAL RESOURCES (PREWAR AND POSTWAR).

Category	Prewar	Postwar	Percentage gain
Coal:			
Production area (sq. km.)	3,880	4,450	15
Number of mines	67	80	19
Production (thousand tons)	32,600	64,650	98
Coke plants	9	20	122
Production (thousand tons)	2,124	5,353	152
Brown coal mines	7	20	186

179

TABLE 63 (*continued*). POLAND'S INDUSTRIAL RESOURCES

Category	Prewar	Postwar	Percentage gain
Production (thousand tons)	18	7,611	3,220
Briquette plants	4	8	100
Production (thousand tons)	17	386	1,270
Zinc and lead:			
Number of mines	2	9	350
Production (thousand tons)	492	1,214	147
Iron ore:			
Number of mines	20	21	5
Production (thousand tons)	792	865	7
Crude oil:			
Number of wells	812	190	—77
Production	501	118	—76
Potassium salts:			
Number of mines	3	0	—
Production (thousand tons)	522	0	—

In addition to the gains listed in Table 63, Poland acquired deposits of cadmium, cobalt, gypsum, and china clay—all of which had had to be imported before the war.

Mere statistics, however, do not bring out the full significance of the changes. When other aspects are taken into account, it can be seen that postwar Poland had an economic potential a good deal higher than that of prewar Poland. As a report by the National Association of Manufacturers states:

Increased resources in zinc ores will now be matched with the large refining capacity formerly separated from the ores by the German-Polish frontier. The chemical industry, in which the gains, measured in workers employed, were not much greater than losses, is now much more diversified and includes plants manufacturing dyes and varnishes, technical oils, fertilizers, etc. Formerly, the industry was largely confined to the production of common consumption goods in wide demand such as soap and matches and to the production of "heavy" chemicals, such as sulphuric acid, caustic soda and superphosphates. The timber losses in the East, coming at the same time as important gains of paper manufacturing plants in the West, have induced Poland to seek timber and cellulose from Finland, Sweden, and USSR.[6]

On balance, we may say, therefore, that, while by the postwar settlement Poland gained slightly in agricultural resources, the country gained substantially in industrial resources. At the same time, however, the industrial potential of the country in terms of capital equipment was considerably below the prewar level, owing to wartime devastation and the removal of capital equipment.

It is noteworthy that Poland made a much quicker economic recovery after World War II than after World War I. If we take the level of Polish industrial production in 1913 as 100, then in 1920 it was only 35.1. If we take the level in 1938 as 100, then in 1946/1947, it was 90.8. If we consider all the countries of Europe which were directly affected by World War II (with the exception of the U.S.S.R.), Poland is, however, pretty far down the list when we range them in order of industrial recovery. By 1946/1947, only Finland, Italy, and Germany (in that order) were below Poland in this respect.

Relative judgments can be very misleading in such cases, however, because they do not take into account the initial level immediately after the war, and the Polish economy had suffered physical destruction probably greater than that of any other European country with the exception of the U.S.S.R. That this low place in the list was primarily the result of the state of the country immediately on the cessation of hostilities is borne out

---

[6] *Economic Potentials behind the Iron Curtain* (New York: National Association of Manufacturers, 1948), pp. 22–23.

by the greatly increased rate of improvement after the immediate postwar years, as shown in Table 64.

TABLE 64. INDEX OF INDUSTRIAL PRODUCTION AND EMPLOYMENT (1947–1949).*

(1948 = 100)		
	Industrial production	Employment in industry
1947	104	120
1948	135	136
1949	166	158

* Postwar figures in postwar territory have been related to prewar figures in prewar territory. *Source:* Extracted from *Economic Bulletin for Europe* (Geneva: U.N. Economic Commission for Europe, 1950), pp. 66 and 68, tables I, VI.

Industrial recovery up to the latter part of 1947 can readily be seen from Table 65.

TABLE 65. INDEX OF INDUSTRIAL PRODUCTION BY INDUSTRIES (JUNE, 1947).*

(1938 = 100)			
Engineering	210	Textiles	95
Electrical power	156	Electrical industries	89
Chemicals	139	Foodstuffs	74
Mining	126	Tobacco	43
Iron and Steel	98	Oil	29
Paper	97	Leather	21

* This table has been constructed from information in various tables in *A Survey of the Economic Situation and Prospects of Europe* (Geneva: U.N. Economic Commission for Europe, 1948).

Perhaps an even better picture of the speed and direction of Poland's industrial recovery may be gathered by looking at the figures for the principal industries, quarter by quarter, during 1946 and 1947. This is done in Table 66, which is based on the same source as Table 65.

182

TABLE 66. INDUSTRIAL PRODUCTION BY INDUSTRIES (1946 AND 1947).
(1938 = 100)

| | 1946 | | | | 1947 | | |
	First quarter	Second quarter	Third quarter	Fourth quarter	First quarter	Second quarter	Third quarter
General index	71	77	80	90	93	100	104
Textiles	82.9	72.7	74.9	87.3	87.7	87.3	97.6
Chemicals	93.7	108.9	114.4	129.7	125.5	141.7	145.2
Iron and steel	68.9	73.8	72.5	80.0	83.8	95.4	99.4
Engineering	86.0	112.3	115.3	143.3	167.0	198.0	190.1
Building	45	85	106	90	44	105	113

The Polish economy by 1947 had passed beyond the stage of immediate first-aid rehabilitation and had embarked on a long-term plan of integrated agricultural and industrial development, reminiscent of Kwiatkowski's Fifteen-Year Plan, which had been cut short by the outbreak of war. Consideration is given later in this chapter to this postwar planning after we have finished this brief factual sketch of economic developments.

It has been mentioned in the preceding chapter that one result of the German invasion of Poland was the almost complete destruction of the banking system. The physical shortage of goods, the destruction of productive equipment, postwar demand for both capital and consumption goods, when added together, resulted in hyperinflation. Although the banking system was nationalized as part of the immediate postwar economic reforms, nationalization alone was no answer to the problem. The government found it necessary to expand the currency in circulation, even though this would have inflationary consequences, as shown in Table 67.

This same phenomenon of hyperinflation, combined with a shortage of money, leading to a further increase in the issue and circulation of currency, had been observed immediately after World War I:

A shortage of money developed sooner or later in all cases of hyperinflation. This paradoxical phenomenon was due to the fact that in

183

TABLE 67. CURRENCY IN CIRCULATION AND COST OF LIVING
(1945–1946).*

	Currency in circulation (zloty)	Cost of living (1937 = 100)
December, 1945	26,300,000	8,950
March, 1946	26,900,000	10,150
June, 1946	36,700,000	11,040
September, 1946	44,500,000	10,650
December, 1946	60,100,000	13,020

* Source: Survey of Current Inflationary and Deflationary Tendencies (New York: U.N. Department of Economic Affairs, 1947), p. 60.

the later stages of inflation the public's anticipations of further note issues and further depreciation pushed up price quotations far in advance of the actual increase in money supplies. The shortage of money then induced an increase in the velocity of circulation which, together with the increase in money supplies, made transactions possible at the inflated level of "anticipatory" price quotations.[7]

The continuance of hyperinflation in the immediate postwar years cannot be considered a fault of the Polish government, which took measures to curb it and stabilize the price level. By 1949 it had succeeded in stabilizing the price level as shown by the cost-of-living index, as may be seen from Table 68. There was a rise at the beginning of 1950—January, 112, and February, 113—but it was clear the inflationary price-wage-price spiral was under control. This conclusion is borne out by a decree of the Council of Ministers of December 30, 1950, which reduced the prices of some important goods effective January 1, 1951: "Prices of certain kinds of fats and meats were reduced by 5 to 10 per cent, soap by 10 per cent, electro-technical and metal goods by 18 to 30 per cent, and window glass by 30 per cent. . . . Prices of a wide range of capital goods, including

[7] The Course and Control of Inflation (League of Nations, 1946), p. 24.

184

TABLE 68. INDEX OF COST OF LIVING (1949).*
(1948 = 100)

1949			
		September	102
January	104	October	103
July	104	November	104
August	102	December	107

* *Source: Economic Bulletin for Europe*, U.N. Economic Commission for Europe, Geneva, 2, No. 1 (July, 1950), p. 51.

machines and railway cars were reduced by 10 to 30 per cent." [8] This reduction in prices was linked with the monetary reform announced by the Polish government October 28, 1950. This reform, put into effect during the week October 31 to November 5, was the issue of a new zloty to be exchanged at the rate of 100 old zloty to one new zloty for private persons and private enterprises, but at a ratio of 100 to 3 for co-operative and state enterprises and for the savings deposits of the working populace. It should be noted that this currency reform had more to it than appears. The finance minister stated that a fundamental objective was "the completion of the process of shifting part of the capital held by capitalists to the masses of workers and peasants." [9] In effect, the real value of the cash balances of private persons, shopkeepers, small industrial enterprises, and farmers were reduced by two-thirds by this measure. The consequences will be that a large part of such private business as remains in Poland will be eliminated, and private farmers, always a recalcitrant group for economic planners to cope with, will become more dependent on state credits and state supplies of machinery and fertilizers, and will thus be "induced" voluntarily to join farming collectives.

In 1945, the government put the banking system under gov-

[8] *International Financial News Survey*, III, No. 27 (1951), 216.

[9] Reported in *Neue Zürcher Zeitung* (Zürich, Switzerland), Nov. 9, 1950. See *International Financial News Survey*, III, No. 22 (1950), 176.

185

ernment control, simplifying its structure and fitting its cash and credit transactions into the needs of the National Credit Plan. This, like the other measures of the time, was emergency action to meet immediate postwar problems. A full-fledged reform, to liquidate the old banking system and prewar accounts and to establish a new long-term structure for Polish banking, was announced, however, by the government at the beginning of 1949. This is described officially as follows:

The present bank reform is designed to streamline the banking system and to nationalize all banks with the following exceptions: small country banks, the Export and Import Bank, which will be conducted on a joint-stock basis, and the cooperative banks. Operating below the county level, there will be three types of credit cooperatives: communal credit cooperatives in rural areas; municipal credit cooperatives, chiefly for the crafts; and employees' cooperative banks, serving the factories.

The number of banks will be reduced to seven, with the jurisdiction of each being kept within strictly defined limits, as follows.

(1) The *National Bank of Poland* will be the central institute, regulating cash and credit circulation and the clearing of domestic and foreign transactions. Within this framework, the National Bank will draw up financial plans, forming part of the overall national economy, and will supervise their execution. The National Bank will finance directly and control government-owned industrial and commercial enterprises, and shortly its operations will also be extended to consumers' cooperatives.

(2) The *Investment Bank* will finance investments, either directly or through the agency of other banks, and exercise control over the use of the invested monies. The Investment Bank, too, will be the sole institute empowered to issue bonds.

(3) A new *Agricultural Bank* is to regulate financial problems in rural areas, extending both long-term and short-term credits.

(4) The *Municipal Bank* will finance the economic enterprises of municipal governments.

186

(5) The *Trade and Commercial Bank* will serve private industry, crafts, trade and working cooperatives. It will, at the same time, supervise local credit cooperatives, in charge of the above activities on a local scale.

(6) The *General Savings Bank* will coordinate nationwide savings and the circulation of checks and money orders.

(7) The *Export and Import Bank* will finance foreign trade.[10]

It will be interesting to see how this carefully planned banking structure works out in practice. It has clearly been designed to make money and credit transactions an integral part of an over-all planning of the economic activities of the country. The changes are more in accord with the totalitarian economic planning of Communist Russia than with the changes that Socialist governments, such as that of Great Britain, have found necessary for making effective their planned economies.

In connection with the monetary and banking reforms, it should be noted that the Polish government cut itself off from international banking by its withdrawal in March, 1950, from the International Monetary Fund. The reasons given for this withdrawal are a good example of the Alice-through-the-Looking Glass attitude toward economic facts of governments behind the Iron Curtain. In the letter of withdrawal, the Polish ambassador to the United States said:

Practice however has shown that the International Monetary Fund has failed to fulfill its duties. The Fund became instead a submissive instrument of the Government of the United States, whose economic and political expansion is in direct contradiction to the purpose to be served by the Fund. Due to its attitude in respect to the selfish policy of the United States Government, the Fund cooperated with the United States Government, which lately forced upon a number of member countries the devaluation of their currencies.

By continuing to be a member of the International Monetary

[10] *Poland of Today*, 4 (March, 1949), 7.

187

Fund, the Polish Government would take upon itself the responsibility for the policy of the Fund, which this Government several times severely and justly criticized in the hope that it would undergo a change.

In view of the above, the Government of the Republic of Poland sees no possibility of continued cooperation with the International Monetary Fund and announces its withdrawal from membership. . . .[11]

Such a travesty of the facts does not warrant an answer as M. Gutt, the then Managing Director and Chairman of the Board of the Fund, observed:

I do not accept the reasons adduced by the Polish Government to explain its reasons for withdrawing, but I do not regard it as necessary to enter into a detailed refutation, inasmuch as the history and actions of the Fund, together with its published statements, particularly its annual reports, are an ample answer to your Government's letter.[12]

Since Poland is in a position to benefit greatly from membership in the International Bank, membership of which is dependent on membership in the International Monetary Fund, this withdrawal was economically stupid from the point of view of the long-run development of the country. It is clear that the voice may have come from Warsaw, but the instructions came from Moscow, and the incident is a sharp indication of the subservience in economic as well as political matters of the present Polish government to that of the U.S.S.R.

The organization of commerce reveals also the same type of totalitarian economic pattern as is to be found in the U.S.S.R. As a recent official source states:

Top planning sales agencies are found necessary to assure the

[11] *Annual Report* (Washington: International Monetary Fund, 1950), pp. 102–103.

[12] *Annual Report* (Washington: International Monetary Fund, 1950), p. 103.

greatest possible advance in the direction of an even and fair distribution of available consumer goods. The goal is to have each community provided with a satisfactory supply of merchandise, with smaller towns served as well as the major cities, additional cost or cut in profits notwithstanding. Such service is a distinct possibility in Poland since distribution and sales are viewed as nothing more than the extension of socialized production. Therefore accounts may be balanced in such a way that certain enterprises unprofitable but indispensable to a community, may be undertaken and continued in operation despite losses. Such losses are counterbalanced by revenues from other activities in the same industry which yield larger returns. . . .

As might be expected, Poland has taken steps to eliminate the middleman who is an important part of the distributive process in many other countries. . . .

Despite advances, there nevertheless remain many difficulties and shortcomings in the development of a highly efficient distribution system in Poland. However, such difficulties face all pioneering efforts and there is widespread confidence that they will be mastered.[13]

This argument for "robbing selected Peter to pay for collective Paul" is drearily familiar, even as to the expression of confidence. The difficulties had better be mastered, or it will be the economics of *Alice in Wonderland* for some unfortunate official: "Off with his head!"

In this connection, it might be asked what has happened to the co-operative movement which played such an important role in the economic life of prewar Poland. It has been both expanded and transformed. The 4,800 retail co-operative outlets of 1938 had become 30,000 outlets by the middle of 1949. Their transformation, however, is a further indication of the dominance of Communist policy in recent developments of the Polish economy. The president of the Central Cooperative Association in Warsaw explains the change in the following words:

[13] *Poland Today,* 5 (Feb., 1950), 13.

Concurrently with the new organizational development, the proper role of cooperatives as integral parts of a socialized economy became more and more clarified. This process was terminated with the full inclusion of cooperatives in the overall economic plan. Henceforth they were to be part and parcel of the nationalized economy, with their production and services clearly defined by an overall plan, and subject to its discipline. The process of clarifying the ideological principles of coops and their role in the construction of a socialist system, involved the overcoming of many erroneous concepts, which encumbered the pre-war ideas about coops and which stemmed from various forms of utopian socialism. . . . To this were added specific errors of the post-war period, such as the theory of an "autonomous sector," independent of the discipline of the overall national economic plan. All these erroneous views were gradually overcome by a self-criticizing ideological growing-up process.

This process of concept revision became especially pronounced in 1948, when in connection with the unification of the labor movement, ideological theories were being generally overhauled, and a clear concept of the road to socialism, based on the theories of Marxism-Leninism, crystallized. In the course of this process, which clarified what further steps our People's democracy was to take, the role of coops in the transformation of our social system became clearly defined.

This role is of a twofold nature. In the first place, cooperatives are an instrument of the class struggle. Together with nationalized business they crowd out private trade and eliminate from the nationalized economy capitalist elements both in the city and in the village. In the second place, coops are instruments in organizing a socialist form of production. They are the best and most efficient means for the socialization of small business. . . .[14]

This language is also familiar—the language of the Russian "purge" trials and of the Nazi *gleichshaltung*. The argument is wholly alien to anything traditionally associated with the cooperative movement, either in prewar Poland or any other non-

[14] Oscar Lange in *Poland of Today,* 4 (Nov., 1949), 17–18.

Socialist country. The name has remained; the substance has disappeared.

The organization of labor unions now also follows the Soviet pattern by embracing all labor and by making the labor unions an integral instrument in a national economic plan. The "co-ordination" of the labor unions was carried through in the summer of 1949 with government authorization and approval of a new central labor union organization, the Federation of Trade Unions. On the surface, the government action would seem a move in the direction of liberal democratic principles. The law guarantees to "manual and white collar workers the right of organization in trade unions and of active participation in the people's government." [15] It further provides for the abolition of all "capitalist regulations still in force, which restrict the right of manual and white collar workers to organize in trade unions, subject union activities to capitalist state supervision, and further the disruption of the trade union movement." These aims sound admirable for the labor unions. The substance of the change is to be found, however, not in the professed aims of the legislation but in the obligations which it imposes on labor union members and in the administrative structure brought into force for carrying the measure into effect. Under the new constitution, members of labor unions have the following obligations: (1) to increase the national wealth by disciplined and conscientious work; (2) to protect the national wealth, which is the property of all working people, and to combat waste; (3) to take an active part in union activities; (4) to pay dues regularly and to maintain union discipline. These are scarcely recognizable principles of voluntary labor unionism to the American or British labor union member, though very recognizable to a member of a Soviet union or to a former member of the Nazi *arbeitsfront*. The individual labor unions are united in the Cen-

[15] *Poland of Today*, 4 (August, 1949), 14, which has been used also for the other references in this paragraph.

191

tral Council of Trade Unions. This centralized governing body has ninety-nine members and thirty-three deputy members, who elect a presidium of twenty-one. From the presidium comes the secretariat, made up of a chairman, three deputy chairmen, and three to six secretaries. There are also district, county, and local councils which co-ordinate union activities within their territories. The parallel to the organization of the Communist Party is easy to follow—"democratic centralism and vertical integration" means a labor movement totally different from the free labor movements of western Europe and the United States. It is not without significance that the first chairman of the Central Council of Trade Unions was Aleksander Zawadzki, who resigned his position as vice-premier of Poland to become leader of the centralized labor unions. As in other sectors of the economy after 1948 the pattern and influence of the Soviet Union becomes increasingly obvious.

That labor unions in Poland could not engage in collective bargaining as understood by Western unions may be seen from the manner in which wages and prices are set by the Polish government. An example of this state determination of real wages was given in the new price and wage policy announced in December, 1949:

At its December 31, 1949 session, the Ministers' Council passed the following resolutions:

(1) As of January 1, 1950, basic hourly and monthly wage rates and additional compensation shall be raised 5 per cent for all employees who draw their pay from state or local government funds and for all those employed in socialized enterprises.

(2) As of January 1, 1950, the family allowance for those whose earnings are within the non-taxable limit, shall be raised 250 zloty monthly for each child.

(3) As of January 1, 1950, the income tax shall be so amended as not to affect the 5 per cent increase granted in resolution (1).

192

(4) As of January 1, 1950,

(a) retail prices of meat and meat products shall be advanced to correspond with prices paid to farmers for livestock;

(b) the prices of certain industrial products shall be revised to cover costs as well as to meet the requirements necessary to a proper development of the national economy.[16]

It was estimated that the wage increase and tax relief would more than cover the effect of the price increase on the working family's cost of living. For the immediate purpose, the interesting thing to note is the unilateral nature of the government's action and its squeeze on those not employed by state organizations, in other words, on the remaining private sector of the economy. Such action is, again, incompatible with the existence of genuinely free labor unions or a genuinely free economy. They are the acts of an economically totalitarian government like that of the U.S.S.R. or of Hitler's Germany.

In the immediate postwar years, as might have been expected from the devastation of the country, Poland's foreign trade was at a very low level and was mainly composed of abnormal relief shipments, as may be seen from Table 69.

TABLE 69. IMPORTS AND EXPORTS (1938 AND 1946/1947).*

	Imports	Exports
	(In U.S. dollars at 1938 prices)	
1938	247,000,000	220,000,000
1946/1947	279,000,000 †	94,000,000

* Source: *Survey of the Economic Situation and Prospects of Europe* (Geneva: Economic Commission for Europe, 1948), p. 37.
† Includes relief shipments.

External assistance, from the end of war through September, 1947, in U.S. dollars at current prices, was as follows: U.N.R.R.A., $577,000,000; U.S.A., $90,000,000; other aid, $114,-

[16] *Poland Today*, 5 (Feb., 1950), 16.

000,000; total, $781,000,000.[17] Thus, in the revival of economic life in Poland, aid from the Western countries, and particularly from the United States, was crucial. Aid from the Soviet Union was negligible in comparison.[18]

With the exception—a very important one—of relief shipments, Poland's foreign trade in 1945 was dominated by her relations with Soviet Russia. In the course of 1946, however, Poland entered into trading relations with the majority of European countries. The new industrialization, like the industrialization of the 1930's, leads to a vital dependence on foreign trade both for industrial raw materials (such as iron ore, cotton, wool, and hides) and for equipment (such as machinery and machine tools). In the period of 1946–1947, Poland's chief export was coal (the most important recipients being the U.S.S.R., Sweden, and Denmark), sugar (to England, Rumania, Switzerland, and the U.S.S.R.), foundry products (to Sweden, Bulgaria, and the U.S.S.R.), textiles, glass, chemical products, and furniture. The major imports were iron ore (from the U.S.S.R. and Sweden), manganese ore (from the U.S.S.R. and Rumania), wool and cotton (from the U.S.S.R. and the U.S.A.), fuel oil (from the U.S.S.R., Hungary, and Germany), cellulose (from Sweden), electrotechnical equipment (from Sweden), and foodstuffs (from a number of countries, headed by the U.S.S.R. and the U.S.A.).

It is now possible to construct a fairly detailed table of the network of Poland's foreign trade for the period after the immediate years of postwar recovery and to compare the pattern with the prewar pattern. This has been done in Table 70.

---

[17] *Salient Features of the World Economic Situation, 1945–47* (New York: U.N. Department of Economic Affairs, 1948), p. 126.

[18] It is necessary to make this dogmatic statement because the current rewriting of history by the Polish authorities, in conformity with Communist practice, states the exact opposite. Factual evidence is precisely the opposite to that required by the party line.

Careful study of Table 70 reveals important changes and an important dilemma for future Polish economic policy. The important change is the growth in trade with the U.S.S.R., which from being a negligible element in 1938 has become the dominant giant in the picture. It should also be noted that there is a definite pattern shown for the trade with the Russian satellites. The very high adverse balance with Soviet Russia is also significant. The dilemma is that trade with non-Communist Europe is still extremely important, both to Poland and to western Europe. Hence, in foreign trade matters Poland has the delicate task of integrating her economy into the pattern of a Russian satellite and in conformity with the U.S.S.R., yet, at the same time, maintaining—and possibly even increasing—trade with western Europe. The pull of economic interest and the pull of political ideology is in diametrically opposed directions. It is perhaps too late to expect that this factor alone can pull Poland out of the Russian orbit, but it is a powerful weapon, which so far has not been used as skillfully as it might have been by the West.

Placed in this difficult position, the Polish government, by using a network of bilateral trade agreements to secure essential imports, has so far shown great skill in its role of Mr. Facing-both-Ways. From January, 1949, to January, 1951, Poland concluded trade agreements in the following order with the following countries: Great Britain, Egypt, Switzerland, Germany (Western Zone), Italy, the U.S.S.R., Czechoslovakia, Finland, Denmark, Bulgaria, Iceland, Albania, Pakistan, Sweden, and France. The Anglo-Polish Trade Agreement of January 14, 1949, was for a period of five years and provided for a steady rise in the trade between the two countries. Britain was to receive important quantities of bacon, eggs, poultry, fish, and fresh fruit. Poland was to receive rubber, wool, and industrial equipment. Under the agreement with Egypt, Poland is to receive cotton and flax in exchange for coal, agricultural products,

195

TABLE 70. NETWORK OF POLAND'S FOREIGN TRADE (VALUED AT CURRENT F.O.B. PRICES IN MILLIONS OF U.S. DOLLARS) (1938, 1948, AND 1949).*

	1938			1948			1949		
	Exports	Imports	Balance	Exports	Imports	Balance	Exports	Imports	Balance
EUROPE:									
Northwestern Europe:									
Austria	11	8	+3	19	3	+16	19	11	+8
Belgium-Luxembourg	10	10	—	8	12	-4	8	12	-4
Denmark	3	2	+1	36	13	+23	29	16	+13
France	9	9	—	32	10	+22	38	35	+3
Germany	44	48	-4	42	31	+11	100	60	+40
Iceland	—	—	—	2	1	+1	3	1	+2
Ireland	—	—	—	—	—	—	1	—	+1
Netherlands	10	7	+3	12	6	+6	25	19	+6
Norway	3	2	+1	19	12	+7	15	13	+2
Sweden	14	9	+5	67	40	+27	47	31	+16
Switzerland	5	5	—	12	8	+4	16	12	+4
United Kingdom	41	26	+15	35	29	+6	50	32	+18
Southern Europe:									
Greece	2	1	+1	—	—	—	—	—	—
Italy	12	6	+6	17	18	-1	31	14	+17
Portugal	1	—	+1	—	—	—	—	—	—
Spain	1	—	+1	—	—	—	—	—	—
Turkey	2	2	—	1	1	—	5	4	+1
U.S.S.R. and Eastern Europe:									
U.S.S.R.	2	3	-1	111	118	-7	135	225	-90
Bulgaria	3	3	—	7	6	+1	12	12	—
Czechoslovakia	8	7	+1	40	53	-13	50	50	—

Finland	4	1	+3	32	8	+24	18	9	+11
Hungary	2	1	+1	4	4	—	12	12	—
Rumania	2	2	—	5	6	—1	13	13	—
Yugoslavia	1	2	—1	22	26	—4	9	5	+4
NORTH AMERICA:									
U.S.A. and dependencies	13	27	—14	1	55	—54	3	23	—20
Canada (including Newfoundland)	—	1	—1	—	6	—6	—	2	—2
LATIN AMERICA:	9	17	—8	3	16	—13	3	15	—12
REST OF WORLD:									
Overseas sterling area	4	20	—16	—	6	—6	2	15	—13
Dependent overseas territories (except British Colonies)	2	7	—5	—	—	—	—	—	—
Other overseas countries	5	5	—	4	10	—6	4	13	—9
SUMMARY:									
Total Europe (including U.S.S.R.)	190	154	+36	523	405	+118	626	586	+40
Total Europe (excluding U.S.S.R.)	188	151	+37	412	287	+125	491	361	+130
Total North America	13	28	—15	1	61	—60	3	25	—22
Total Latin America	9	17	—8	3	16	—13	3	15	—12
Total rest of world (as above)	11	32	—21	4	16	—12	6	28	—22
GRAND WORLD TOTAL:	223	231	—8	531	498	+33	638	654	—16

* These figures are the result of adjustments intended to reconcile the official data reported by both trade partners concerned. They do not, therefore, necessarily agree with the official figures published by any one government.
— indicates nil or less than one-half million dollars.

The raw data, which have been rearranged and from which the balances have been calculated, are taken from Table XXI in Economic Commission for Europe (Geneva), *Economic Bulletin for Europe*, Vol. 2, No. 2, October, 1950. Pages 86 to 89 of this *Bulletin* should be consulted for details on the statistical methods used to compile the import and export figures.

chemicals, locomotives and rolling stock, and glass. The agreement with Switzerland was for five years, and Poland was to receive capital equipment, dyes, medical supplies, and watches, in exchange for coal, agricultural produce, chemicals, and textiles. The agreement with Germany (Western Zone) was for only one year. Poland was to export grain, sugar, vegetables, paper, and porcelain and receive in exchange machines and industrial equipment, optical and precision instruments, chemicals, metal products, and minerals. The agreement with Italy was to be for the exchange of coal, grain, timber, and chemicals in return for mineral ores, dyes, machines, tires, hemp, and citrus fruits. The agreements with the U.S.S.R., Czechoslovakia, and Finland were interconnected:

(1) Finland is to supply the U.S.S.R. with prefabricated houses, building material, and small ships, to the amount of 100 million rubles;

(2) the U.S.S.R. is to ship to Poland foodstuffs totaling 80 million rubles, and to Czechoslovakia, 20 million rubles;

(3) Poland is to export to Finland 80 million rubles' worth of coal, while Czechoslovakia will furnish Finland with sugar, machines, and other products to the sum of 20 million rubles.[19]

In January, 1950, a protocol was signed to the agreement between Poland and the U.S.S.R. providing for a 34-per-cent increase in total trade in 1950 over 1949. The main items of Polish exports to Russia were to be coal, railroad rolling stock, iron and other metals, textiles, and sugar. The main items to be received from Russia in exchange were cotton, iron ore, manganese ore, chrome ore, cars, tractors, agricultural machinery, mineral oil products, chemicals, and foodstuffs. After the lapse of the existing trade agreement with France at the end of 1949, trade between the two countries dropped considerably. A short-run agreement was signed in January, 1951, which would increase the trade between France and Poland. Exports from Poland to

[19] *Poland of Today,* 4 (August, 1949), 17.

France were to be principally coal, agricultural products, and textiles, in exchange for iron and steel, iron ore, automobile parts, and chemicals. This short summary of the principal recent bilateral deals is enough to show the significance of non-Communist countries in the Polish trade pattern even after the greater part of the Polish economy had been planned on the Russian model and integrated as far as possible with the economies of the U.S.S.R. and its satellites.

In connection with such a pattern of bilateral deals, it is only to be expected that rigid exchange control will be found. Until late in 1950, the Polish government relied on the decree of April 26, 1936, an inheritance from the prewar regime. At the time of the monetary reform of October, 1950, however, this prewar decree was strengthened. It had forbidden transactions in foreign exchange. The decree which replaced it in October, 1950, made in addition the mere *possession* of foreign exchange an offense. Under the new decree all foreign exchange and gold coins must be sold to, or deposited with, the National Bank of Poland.

In these circumstances, foreign exchange rates are almost completely meaningless. The currency reform of October 28, 1950, did, however, define the zloty as being worth 0.222168 grains of fine gold. This made the exchange rate: 1 zloty = 1 rouble of 4 zloty = 1 U.S. dollar. This rate overvalues the zloty against the U.S. dollar and most western European currencies but undervalues it as against the Russian rouble. This formal linking of the zloty to gold, however, is largely devoid of significance, since no foreign country is able to exchange zloty for gold. Moreover, trade transactions covered by trade agreements are carried out in terms of negotiated prices, corresponding roughly to world market prices. Thus, each international transaction carries virtually its own exchange rate for the zloty.

After this survey of the factual achievements of the Polish economy in the period to the end of 1949, and in some instances

199

into 1950, it is appropriate to consider the conscious economic plans of the Polish government and how far they were carried out. The new government had adopted preliminary economic plans as early as 1945. The first full-dress plan was the Three-Year Plan, adopted in provisional form in September, 1946, and approved in its final definitive form in July, 1947. It was to cover the years 1947, 1948, and 1949. The general goal of the plan was within that period to make definite structural changes in the Polish economy as well as to carry out at the same time industrial rehabilitation and reconstruction. In particular the aim was to increase the share in the national economy of industry, devoting particular attention to the development of mining, transport, the production of agricultural machinery (especially tractors), of electric power and electrical installations, and of transport equipment. The plan as a whole showed a nice balancing of the immediate social and economic needs to increase consumption with the need at the same time to maintain a high level of capital investment. It was hoped to raise the average per capita consumption of foodstuffs and manufactured goods to the 1938 level in the third year of the plan and to exceed it in the fourth year (except for agricultural products, which would remain at the 1938 level). At the same time it was planned to have a capital investment program of approximately 20 per cent of the national income. These were steep objectives, particularly in respect to agriculture, when we recall that in 1945 agricultural production was only at 45 per cent of the 1938 level.

One of the foundations of the plan was the economic integration of the new territories gained by Poland in the west with the remainder of the country. In this connection, a planned migration of surplus population from the old territories into the new areas was an important feature. The main objectives, apart from migration, of the planned economic integration of the new Poland were four:

200

(1) An even distribution of rural and urban population throughout the whole of the country;

(2) The development of industry to meet the needs of the whole country;

(3) The creation of a homogeneous system of agriculture for the whole country;

(4) The linking of the old and new territories by a uniform transport network.

The long-range objective of the plan may be judged from the following extract:

[The goal is] to raise the living standard of the working masses above the pre-war level. This shall be accomplished through reconstruction to make good wartime losses and by introducing new principles of economic and social organization; also through the economic unification of the regained territories with the old.

The Plan recommends especially emphasis on the development of those branches of the national economy which, while not directly filling immediate consumption needs, are nevertheless indispensable for the future growth of the production of consumer goods, namely:

(a) The production of agricultural implements, machinery and fertilizers, to be developed according to market needs.

(b) The production of coal, a decisive factor in Poland's export potential, must be developed to the maximum of its possibilities.

(c) The production of electric energy and the electrification of the country at large shall, in view of their importance to all other spheres of production, have unqualified priority in matters of investment policy.

(d) Transportation shall, for the duration of the Plan, have first place in questions of determining *amounts* of investment.[20]

It will be seen that, if these objectives could be achieved, the new Poland would have gone a very long way indeed toward

---

[20] *Rehabilitation of Polish Economy* (New York: Polish Research and Information Service, 1948), p. 3.

finding a solution of the major economic problems which harassed the country throughout the twenty years from 1919 to 1939.

Since the immediate need of the country was raising the level of consumption to a standard of minimum decency, the plan laid down certain priorities for the production of consumer goods. The order of priority was as follows:

(1) staple foodstuffs;

(2) necessary footwear, textiles, and clothing;

(3) industrial articles for household use;

(4) other consumer goods.

The Polish government claims that the Three-Year Plan was successfully accomplished:

Within 2 years and 10 months the Three Year Plan had been carried out 100.6 per cent, . . . living standards, as compared with 1946, have gone up generally and, in some fields, they even exceed pre-war levels. . . . If the people of Poland are better fed and dressed in 1949 than they were before the war, it is due primarily to the rise in industrial production, which is now two and a half the pre-war level. . . . Polish industry now produces almost 75 per cent more than before the war, and heavy industry in particular shows great production increases. . . .

Agricultural output in 1946 was 4.6 billion zlotys as against 7.8 billions in 1949. Per capita production has risen 112–115 per cent as compared with pre-war. . . .[21]

It is possible to make a rough check on these claims by using the monthly average figures given by the Research and Planning Division of the Economic Commission for Europe in the various issues of the *Economic Bulletin for Europe*. The government's claims seem somewhat exaggerated, but not greatly so. They seem least exaggerated in respect to the increase in industrial productivity. The planned hard-coal production for 1949 was 77.5 million tons; actual production was approximately 74.04

[21] *Poland Today*, 5 (Jan., 1950), 3.

million tons. The planned production of electrical energy was 8,400 million kw.-h.; actual production was approximately 8,040 million kw.-h. The planned output of steel was 2,033 thousand tons; actual output was approximately 2,304 thousand tons. In general, therefore, the author is inclined to believe the Polish government's claim for the general success of the Three-Year Plan, although he does not accept the accuracy of their claims in certain sectors.

The Polish government gives as the main reasons for the success of the plan the measures of socialization carried out in the period:

There are several reasons. One is the growth of the nationalized sector of industry which today comprises almost 90 per cent of the nation's factory output and, as is well known, government enterprise is guided by the needs of the people and not, like capitalist production, by the profit motive. Another reason is the development of nationalized and cooperative trade which, in the wholesale division, comprises 60 per cent of Poland's overall trade. A third reason is the planned regulation of farming. . . . The growing movement of labor competition is another factor . . . to which should be added the support of new methods and inventions devised by the workers themselves, and the promotion of outstanding experts among the rank and file to managerial positions.[22]

It would be difficult to dispute these reasons, if only because we do not know what production would have been under other conditions. In this connection, however, it is pertinent to note that the government inherited a tradition of successful economic planning, at least in the industrial sector of the economy, from the prewar governments. One very important factor is, moreover, missing from the official list of reasons and that is the acquisition by Poland of the highly developed industrial area between the Vistula and the Neisse-Oder frontier and of the improved

[22] *Poland Today*, 5 (Jan., 1950), 4.

position in regard to material and natural resources resulting from these acquisitions.

The Three-Year Plan has been followed by a Six-Year Plan. The general nature and aims of this plan were described by Hilary Minc, Ministry of Industry and Commerce, in a speech on December 19, 1948, to the United Polish Workers Party Congress. He stated:

> The goal of our second plan is the development and economic transformation of the country. . . .
>
> Basically the plan is designed to lay the foundations of socialism in Poland, and that means:
>
> (1) A marked increase of our productive capacity, with the stress laid on capital goods production;
>
> (2) Restriction of capitalist elements, depriving them of major influence in any sector of our economy;
>
> (3) Definite steps in the direction of a voluntary socialization of the retail trade, thereby bringing a gradual halt to capitalist expansion;
>
> (4) Substantial improvement in material welfare, better living standards, and higher cultural levels for the working population. . . .
>
> Since industrialization is the basic goal of the Six Year Plan, it is obvious that the scales will gradually tip in favor of industry as against agriculture. Although agricultural production will increase as such, the tempo will be slower than in industry. However, the disparity should not be too pronounced, or else industrial production will be crucially handicapped. . . . Agriculture must therefore follow the pace of industry so as to assure higher consumption levels. . . . Agriculture must therefore keep abreast of industry, so as to assure this increased supply of agricultural raw materials. . . . Our growing industry will call for more and more machinery and raw materials that must be imported from abroad. To cover the costs of these imports we will have to export our own products, among them those of agriculture. Agriculture, therefore, must keep in step with industry to assure surplus products for export. . . .[23]

[23] *Poland of Today,* 4 (Feb., 1949), 16–19.

Quantitatively, the goals of the new plan were first announced in a directive from the Council of Ministers on May 30, 1949. In general terms, the declared aim was that industrial production in 1955 should be 214 per cent of 1949 and agricultural production 145 per cent of 1949. Emphasis in agriculture was to be on developing livestock rather than crops. In basic industrial materials the goals were declared to be as shown in Table 71.

TABLE 71. PRODUCTION GOALS OF THE SIX-YEAR PLAN FOR 1955.*

	Production, 1938	Production target, 1955
Electric power	4,000,000,000 kw.h.	18,000,000,000 kw.-h.
Coal	38,000,000 tons	95,000,000 tons
Cement	2,000,000 tons	4,000,000 tons
Steel ingots	1,500,000 tons	4,000,000 tons
Sulphuric acid	289,000 tons	560,000 tons

* *Source:* Figures taken from *Poland of Today*, 4 (August, 1949), 3.

Production called for in this plan was to exceed 1949's by the following percentages:

Wheat	44
Rye	28
Potatoes	15
Sugar beets	28
Cattle	51
Hogs	59
Sheep	56
Meat production	76
Milk	100+
Agricultural machinery	183
Fertilizers	119

These goals and targets became legally operative on July 21, 1950, when the *Sejm* (Polish legislative assembly) unanimously adopted the Six-Year Plan. In so doing, the noneconomic aspects of the plan were strongly emphasized. President Boleslaw Bierut declared: "It would be erroneous to see in it only the external, quantitative aspect. . . . The Six Year Plan is not only an economic program but also an ideological, political and social program. It is a plan to create strong and unshakable foundations of a new social regime in Poland, the foundations of socialism." [24] It is as yet too early to say what success the Polish government will have with the new plan. Judging from past performance, the author will be surprised if they fall very far short of it. There is some evidence that progress is going along much as expected. With regard to socialization, it was reported in March, 1951:

About 80 per cent of the [government] revenue is planned to originate [for 1951] from the socialized sector of the economy, i.e., from state and cooperative establishments. (Ninety-six per cent of industry, almost the entire wholesale trade, about 85 per cent of organized retail trade, all transportation and communication, and about 13 per cent of agricultural production are nationalized or functioning as cooperatives.) A little less than 41 per cent (about 21.2 billion zlotys) of total expenditures is to be spent on the socialized economy, 31.6 per cent (about 16.4 billion) for social and cultural purposes, 11.6 per cent (about 6 billion) on administration and justice, and 7.2 per cent (about 3.7 billion) on national defense. . . .[25]

There is some indication, however, that the plan is running into difficulties because of a shortage of industrial labor, owing to the difficulty of inducing labor to move from the rural areas into the towns. This problem, of course, in a socialist economy may be overcome by coercion, and there are already hints that the recalcitrant peasantry will meet with the same treatment as the

---

[24] Quoted in *Poland Today*, 5 (Sept., 1950), 3.
[25] *International Financial News Survey*, III, No. 36 (1951), 287.

Russian kulaks. Mr. Minc is reported as having said: "We have become familiarized with the Bolshevist method of planning, tried and tested in the victorious socialist construction in the Soviet Union." He stated that the change from "small, dispersed individual peasant industry" to the "socialist team industry" would be voluntary, but he also added that the government would "continue the policy of restricting, driving out, and then liquidating the rural capitalists as a class." [26] Such difficulties, however, need not prevent the accomplishment of planned objectives if the planners are sufficiently ruthless.

Perhaps that is the right note on which to end this small book. The author has tried to avoid taking sides in dealing with a highly controversial area: he prefers to let the record speak for itself as far as possible. He has tried to show clearly the very great accomplishments of the Polish economy in the years between the two world wars, then the devastation of the country, and finally the very great achievements in the years between 1945 and 1950. The years between the wars were marked by an increasing tendency towards *étatism* and a planned economy. It seemed that in these years Poland was evolving a model of what is sometimes termed a "mixed" economy, part socialist, part private enterprise. The experiment was cut short by the German and Russian invasions of late 1939. After World War II, the Polish economy wavered for a short time between East and West and finally settled for inclusion in the Soviet orbit. There can be no doubt that Poland today is a thoroughgoing totalitarian economy based in theory and practice on the best Soviet models. That is a tragedy for Poland and for the rest of Europe. Nevertheless, because of its economic needs for machinery and industrial raw materials Poland cannot shut itself off from the West but must rely on a substantial volume of trade with the

[26] Information on rural labor difficulties taken from the London *Times* (weekly ed.), Oct. 18, 1950, p. 2.

Western powers. In that connection, there may be hope. In any event, no matter what one's personal ideology may be, it is impossible to deny the very great economic achievements of the Polish people and successive Polish governments both in the years between the wars and in the years after 1945.

Bibliography

[This reading list is not intended to be an exhaustive bibliography of the subject. It includes almost all the sources easily available in English which were used by the author. It does not include books in French, German, or Polish, because students of the subject will be familiar with the more important ones, and the ordinary reader will almost certainly not wish to use them.]

Baginski, H. *Poland and the Baltic*. Oliver and Boyd, London, 1942.

Barański, Leon. *Some Economic Problems of Poland*. Lecture delivered in London to a Conference of School Teachers, March 21, 1943.

Bor-Komorowski, T. *The Secret Army*. Macmillan Company, New York, 1951.

Buell, R. L. *Poland: Key to Europe*. Jonathan Cape, London, 1939.

Dewey, C. S. *Combined Reprint of the Quarterly Reports of the Financial Adviser to the Polish Government*. Printing Office of the Bank of Poland, Warsaw, 1930.

Dyboski, R. *Poland*. Ernest Benn, London, 1933.

Gorecki, R. *Poland and Her Economic Development*. Allen and Unwin, London, 1935.

Jerram, C. B. *Report on Economic and Commercial Conditions in Poland*. Department of Overseas Trade, London, 1937.

Kagan, George. "The Agrarian Régime of Pre-War Poland" in *Journal of Central European Affairs*, October, 1943.

Kemmerer, E. W. *Reports*. Ministry of Finance, Warsaw, 1926.

Kirk, Dudley. *Europe's Population in the Interwar Years*. League of Nations, 1946.

Kozicki, S. *The Social Evolution of Poland in the Nineteenth Century*. London, 1918. Lectures delivered at University College, London.

Kruszewski, Charles. "The German-Polish Tariff War (1925–34) and Its Aftermath" in *Journal of Central European Affairs*, October, 1943.

Machray, R. *The Poland of Pilsudski*. Allen and Unwin, London, 1936.

Maynard, Sir John. *The Russian Peasant and Other Studies*. Victor Gollancz, Ltd., London, 1942.

Minc, Hilary. *Poland's Economy: Present and Future*. Polish Research and Information Service, New York, 1949.

Moore, Wilbert E. *Economic Demography of Eastern and Southern Europe*. League of Nations, Geneva, 1945.

Newman, B. *New Frontiers of Europe*. Hutchinson, London.

Newman, B. *Russia's Neighbour—The New Poland*. Victor Gollancz, Ltd., London, 1946.

Notestein, Frank W. *et al. The Future Population of Europe and the Soviet Union*. League of Nations, Geneva, 1944.

Ponikowska, M. L., and Jurkowa, M. *Polish Youth*. Committee of Polish Students in Great Britain, London, 1942.

Rakowski, J. *The Polish Central Industrial Zone Scheme*. The Baltic Institute, Gdynia, 1938.

Retinger, J. H. *All about Poland*. Minerva Publishing Company, London, 1941.

Rose, William J. *Poland*. Penguin Books, London, 1939.

Rose, William J. (trans.). *From Serfdom to Self-Government: Memoirs of a Polish Village Mayor, 1842–1927*. Minerva Publishing Company, London, 1941.

Russell, Sir John. "Reconstruction and Development in Eastern Poland, 1930–39" in *Geographical Journal*, XCVIII, Nos. 5, 6.

Rybczynski, M. *The Pomeranian Vistula*. Torun, 1934.

Schwartz, Harry. *Russia's Soviet Economy*. Prentice-Hall, Inc., New York, 1950.

Segal, Simon. *Nazi Rule in Poland*. Robert Hale, London, 1943.

Seton-Watson, Hugh. *Eastern Europe between the Wars.* Cambridge University Press, Cambridge, England, 1945.

Seton-Watson, Hugh. *The East European Revolution.* London, Methuen, 1950.

Smogorzewski, C. *Poland's Access to the Sea.* Allen and Unwin, London, 1938.

Sweezy, Paul M. *Socialism,* McGraw-Hill Book Co., Inc., New York, 1949. (Ch. 4, "Socialism in Eastern Europe.")

Szumski, Romuald. *Labor and the Soviet System.* New York, National Committee for a Free Europe, Inc., 1951. [Useful for account of treatment of Polish labor unions and labor leaders under the Communist regime.]

Tallents, Sir Stephen. *Man and Boy.* Faber and Faber, Ltd., London, 1943.

Taylor, J. "The Economic Problems of Poland, 1919 to 1939" in *Young Britain Looks at Poland,* ed. William J. Rose. Anglo-Polish Society, London, 1944.

Truszkowski, A. *Poland To-day.* Warsaw, 1939.

Wajnryb, Miesczslaw. "The Economic and Social Importance of the Central Industrial District of Poland" in *International Labor Review,* I.L.O., November, 1938.

Wanklyn, H. G. *The Eastern Marchlands of Europe.* George Philip, London, 1941.

Warriner, Doreen. *Revolution in Eastern Europe.* Turnstile Press, London, 1950.

Wellisz, Leopold. *Foreign Capital in Poland.* Allen and Unwin, London, 1938.

Zwaleska, Z. *The Welfare of Mothers and Children in Poland.* London [n.d.].

Zweig, F. *The Planning of Free Societies.* Secker & Warburg, London, 1942.

Zweig, F. *Poland between Two Wars.* Secker & Warburg, London, 1944.

OFFICIAL PUBLICATIONS: PREWAR POLISH GOVERNMENT

Concise Statistical Year-Book of Poland. Polish Ministry of Information, London, 1941.

211

Polish-Soviet Relations, 1918–1943. Polish Embassy, Washington, D.C.

Memorandum Handed to the British and American Governments on January 22nd. 1945 and *Declaration of the Polish Government concerning the Decisions Taken with Regard to Poland at the Crimea Conference.* Polish Ministry of Information, February, 1945.

OFFICIAL PUBLICATIONS: POSTWAR POLISH GOVERNMENT

Poland Today (formerly *Poland of Today*). Polish Research and Information Service, New York. (Monthly magazine.)

Land Reform. Polish Research and Information Service, New York, n.d. (Short memorandum.)

Poland's Recovery. Polish Research and Information Service, New York, n.d. (Printed broadsheet.)

Poland's World Trade. Polish Research and Information Service, New York, n.d. (Printed broadsheet.)

Rehabilitation of Polish Economy. Polish Research and Information Service, New York, 1948.

ANONYMOUS AUTHORSHIP

Poland: Human and Economic Characteristics in Their Geographic Setting. ("University of Birmingham Information Service on Slavonic Countries," Monograph No. 1.) Birmingham, England, 1936.

The National Income of Poland. ("University of Birmingham Information Service on Slavonic Countries," Monograph No. 4.) Birmingham, England, 1937.

The Co-operative Movement in Poland. Co-operative Research Institute, Warsaw, 1936.

Contemporary Poland (3d ed.). Central European Times Publishing Company, Zurich, 1938. (Reprint of the chapter "Poland" in *Handbook of Central and East Europe,* 1938.)

Workers' Protective Legislation in Poland. London, 1941.

Eastern Poland. Polish Research Centre, London, 1941.

"Polish-British Economic Co-operation" in *Poland of To-morrow.* London, May 20, 1942.

BIBLIOGRAPHY

The Penetration of German Capital into Europe. Inter-Allied Information Committee, London, 1942.

"The Polish Co-operative Movement" in *Polish Fortnightly Review* (London), Oct. 15, 1943.

"The Economic Situation in Poland" in *Polish Fortnightly Review* (London), Jan. 15, 1943.

Food Consumption Levels in the U.S., Canada, and the U.K. Report of a Special Joint Committee Set Up by the Combined Food Board, H.M.S.O., London, 1944.

Trade and Trade Policies behind the Iron Curtain. Research Department, National Association of Manufacturers, New York, 1948.

Economic Potentials behind the Iron Curtain. Research Department, National Association of Manufacturers, New York, 1948.

"Polish Programme" in London *Times* (weekly ed.), Oct. 18, 1950. (Editorial.)

LEAGUE OF NATIONS REPORTS

Statistical Year-Book. (Annual issues.)

World Economic Survey. (Annual issues.)

The Course and Phases of the World Economic Depression. Geneva, 1931.

Poland. (European Conference on Rural Life, Publication No. 29, 1940.)

Europe's Trade. Geneva, 1941.

The Network of World Trade. Geneva, 1942.

International Currency Experience. 1944.

Money and Banking, 1942/44. Geneva, 1945.

Course and Control of Inflation. 1946.

Food, Famine, and Relief. Geneva, 1946.

UNITED NATIONS: OFFICIAL REPORTS

Statistical Yearbook, 1949–50. New York, 1950.

International Financial News Survey. International Monetary Fund, Washington, D.C. (Weekly.)

World Food Survey. F.A.O., Washington, D.C., 1946.

213

Survey of Current Inflationary and Deflationary Tendencies. Department of Economic Affairs, New York, 1947.

Economic Development in Selected Countries. Department of Economic Affairs, New York, 1947.

Salient Features of the World Economic Situation, 1945–47. Department of Economic Affairs, New York, 1948.

A Survey of the Economic Situation and Prospects of Europe. Research and Planning Division, Economic Commission for Europe, Geneva, 1948.

Report of Mission to Poland, 1947. F.A.O., Washington, D.C., 1948.

Balance of Payments Yearbook, 1938, 1946, 1947. I.M.F., Washington, D.C., 1949.

Economic Bulletin for Europe. Research and Planning Division, Economic Commission for Europe, 1949——.

Annual Report. I.M.F., Washington, D.C., 1950.

Direction of International Trade, Jan.–Dec., 1950. ("Statistical Papers Series T, Vol. I, No. 9.") U.N. Statistical Office, New York, April, 1951.

Population and Vital Statistics Reports. ("Statistical Papers, Series A, Vol. III, No. 1.") New York, 1951.

Index

Acceptance Bank, 55

Agrarian population, distribution by status, 69

Agrarian Reform Act, 1920, 73

Agricultural Association, 1850–1860, 9

Agricultural Bank, 1949, 186

Agricultural co-operatives, 108

Agricultural earnings, 69, 70

Agricultural exports, 78, 120

Agricultural production after 1942, 162, 174

Agricultural prosperity, dynamic relation to whole economy, 62

Agricultural reform, 73, 77, 148, 149

Agricultural Union of Cooperatives, membership, 1937, 110

Agricultural wages, 70, 71

Agriculture: Central Lowlands, 15; devastation, 1939–1943, 161, 173; of Eastern Poland after 1941, 161; under Nazi occupation, 160; of Prussian Poland, 10; regional differences in, 64; in war years, 1914–1920, 12

Agriculture and Land Reforms, Ministry of, 1944, 174

Air services, 21

Anglo-Polish Trade Agreement, 1949, 195

Arable area, 1945, 173

Arable land, decline in uncultivated, 1945–1948, 177

Area of Poland: 1772 and 1919, 4; 1919–1939, 13; 1951, 13

Austrian Poland: economic policy, 10; oil boom, 11; self-government, 10

Bank of National Economy, 37; capital, 50; credit policy, 50; deposits, 1928–1938, 55

Bank of Poland, 1924, 38; assets and liabilities, 49; credit policy, 49; deposits, 1928–1938, 55; note issue, 49-50

Banking: concentration, 54; under Nazi occupation, 159; reconstruction under Grabski, 47; reforms, 1949, 186; system, government control, 185-186

Banking Law of 1928, 47

Barley, area sown, 1938 and 1949, 177

Belgium, commercial treaty, 119

217

Forests, nationalization of, 1944, 174
Four-Year Plan, 1936, 48
France: exports to, 199; trade agreement with, 198
Frontiers, vulnerability of presenting economic difficulties, 14
Furniture, exports, 1946–1947, 194

Gdynia, 122, 123
General Savings Bank, 1949, 187
German Co-operatives, 112
German "New Order," 166, 167
Germany: customs war with, 32; immigrants from, end of nineteenth century, 9; industrial areas of ceded to Poland, 1945, 179; invasion of Poland by, 1939, 157; migration of Germans to Poland, 158; railway policy of, 11; tariff war with, 117, 118; territorial gains from, 1945, 173, 174; trade agreement with, 1934, 119
Government-in-exile, plans for land reform by, 175
Government-General, 165; Bank of Issue, 159; food consumption, 163
Grabski, W., financial reforms of, 1924, 37, 144

Hanseatic League, 5
Hapsburgs, economic policy, 10
Haupttreuhandstelle Ost, 165
Health insurance, 135
Hermann Goering Werke, 165
Highways, 20
Holidays with pay, 134
Housing, public assistance to, 88
Hydroelectric developments, 17
Hyperinflation, 183

Imports: high proportion of industrial raw materials in, 119; mediaeval, 5; in 1938 and 1946/1947, 193
Income consumed, 1929, 125; per head, 70
Industrial areas gained from Germany, 1945, 179
Industrial development, 82; effect of Grabski's financial reforms on, 83; effect of world economic crisis on, 83
Industrial investment, as percentage of national income, 90
Industrial production: 1922–1939, 91; by industries, 1946 and 1947, 182, 183
Industrial recovery: after 1936, 83; 1921–1931, 90; trend after 1919, 83
Industrial resources, prewar and postwar, 179
Industrialization: retarded by low level of voluntary savings, 33; uneven regional distribution, 83
Industries, by number of workers, 84
Inflation, postwar, 184
Inowroclaw, salt deposits, 15
Insurrections: of 1830–1831, 9; of 1863, 9
International Labor Organization, Polish participation in, 131
International Monetary Fund, Polish withdrawal from March, 1950, 187
Investment Bank, the, 1949, 186
Investment in industry, as percentage of national income, 90
Iron ore: deficiency in, 81; imports of, 1946–1947, 194; prewar and postwar position in, 180
Iron and steel, 1946–1947, 183

Motor traffic, 21
Municipal Bank, 1949, 186

Napoleon, influence of, 8
National Bank of Poland, 1949, 186
National income: distribution, 1929,
30, 126; per head, 70
National Land Bank: capital, 51;
deposits, 1928–1938, 55; founda-
tion of, 51; purposes and policy,
51
National Land Fund, 1944, 174
National Liberation, Committee of,
1944, 168
National Unity, Government of, 171
Nationalization of forests, 1944, 174
Natural increase in population, 22
Neisse-Oder frontier, 173
Net reproduction rate, 26
Netherlands, tariff protocol with,
119
"New Order," German, 166, 167
Nutrients per person, 1945–1948,
178
Nutrition, standard of, 127

Oats, area sown in, 1938 and 1949,
177
Oil: boom, Austrian Poland, 11;
fields, 19; imports of, 1946–1947,
194; production of, prewar and
postwar, 180
Overpopulation, rural, 22, 72

Partitions: effects on economic development, 11; Fifth, 169; First,
1772, 7; Fourth, 157, 158; imper-
fect industrialization under, 30;
Second, 1793, 8; Third, 1795, 8
Peasants: coercion of under Six-Year
Plan, 207; conditions of, 1945–
1947, 173; standard of living, 68,
69, 71, 124, 126

Petroleum production, 79
Polesie, planned economic development of, 1931, 16
Polish Corridor, disappearance of,
173
Polish-Soviet agreement, 1941, 168
Pomorze, Union of Rural Co-operatives in, 112
Poniatowski, Stanislas Augustus, 8
Population, 22; density in Central
Lowlands, 14; dependent on agriculture, 24, 63; dependent on industry, 83; natural increase of,
22; net reproduction rate of, 26;
1931 and 1939, 22; occupational
distribution of, 61; prewar and
postwar, 172; problems, 142;
rural bias of, 24, 143; surplus
agricultural, 77; table by coun-
tries, 23
Post Office Savings Bank, 38;
growth of deposits, 52
Potassium salts, 81; prewar and
postwar, 180
Potatoes: area sown, 1938 and 1949,
177; production of, 66
Potsdam conference, 1945, 172
Price control, 1937, 106
Price and wage policy, 1949, 192
Printing industry, 89
Produce exchanges, 105
Production, industrial, 1947–1949,
182
Prussian economic policy, 7, 9, 10
Prussian Poland, agriculture, 10
Public works, 130

Railroads: 1834–1848, 19; comparative statistics, 20; German policy
on, 11; Katowice to Gdynia, 21;
1918–1936, 20; Russian Poland,
3
Real wages, 1928–1936, 128